Eamon Evans is the author of ten vaguely funny books and an unfinished Masters thesis. He lives in Melbourne and probably gets tanked a touch more than he should.

Published by Affirm Press in 2017
28 Thistlethwaite Street, South Melbourne, VIC 3205.
www.affirmpress.com.au

Copyright © Eamon Evans, 2017
All rights reserved. No part of this publication may be reproduced without prior permission of the publisher.

National Library of Australia Cataloguing-in-Publication entry available for this title at www.nla.gov.au

Title: Tanked / Eamon Evans, author.
ISBN: 9781925475722 (paperback)

Cover Design: Nanette Backhouse, saso.creative
Cover photograph: Bill Bachman / Alamy Stock Photo
Typesetting and internal design by Post Pre-press Group
Proudly printed in Australia by Griffin Press

The paper this book is printed on is certified against the Forest Stewardship Council® Standards. Griffin Press holds FSC chain of custody certification SGS-COC-005088. FSC promotes environmentally responsible, socially beneficial and economically viable management of the world's forests.

All reasonable effort has been made to attribute copyright and credit. Any new information supplied will be included in subsequent editions.

TANKED

HOW GETTING WASTED HELPED SHAPE HISTORY

EAMON EVANS

CONTENTS

THIRST-QUENCHERS — 5
Beer, wine & spirits

MIND-BENDERS — 135
Mushrooms, plants & LSD

HEART-STARTERS — 191
Amphetamines & cocaine

CHILLAXANTS — 241
Opium, heroin & dope

INTRODUCTION

'Man, being reasonable, must get drunk. The best of life is but intoxication.'

Lord Byron

Once upon a time I was a boy of 18: bright-eyed, bushy-tailed, lightly pimpled. I had the beginnings of a goatee and some green-and-red hippie pants, stupidly long hair and a new pack of rollies. I had bought a book by Michel Foucault and very nearly read a whole chapter, and was doing my best to like music that did not have a tune. I was more of a feminist than any female I knew, and more than happy to tell them all why – just after I'd finished explaining racism to migrants.

In other words, I was all set for uni.

My subject of choice was History, of course. (Or 'Herstory', as I may well have called it.) I mean, why on earth would you study anything else? War and peace, murders and suicides, revolutions and riots, tights and ruffs – to me, it sounded far more fun than torts, and all that other dreck they dish up in a law degree.

But here's the thing: it wasn't at all. History – as taught at uni, at least – turned out to be all about idiotically complicated theories instead of fun, racy facts. It wasn't enough to know what stuff had happened, we were expected to understand *why*. If I was to tell you that in our first semester we were taught 'parametric determinism', 'cultural materialism' and the 'theory of historical trajectory', I think you would agree that we suffered.

Anyway, I've forgotten that stuff now. I'll probably be able to tell a psychiatrist all about Hegel's 'dialectical method' 30 years from now, but for the time being it remains safely suppressed, somewhere deep inside my subconscious.

But what I *do* remember is this: crudely speaking, there are two basic theories of history, two broad and unifying explanations for why humans do what they do, from which all the more complicated theories derive.

The first is what's known as the 'Great Man Theory'. Essentially, it just means that history was made by a small handful of people – generally men – each of whom was in some way exceptional. It's the idea that the Roman Empire would never have happened without Julius Caesar, for example, or that there wouldn't have been a Russian Revolution without Trotsky and Lenin. Individual intelligence, individual charisma, individual goodness, individual evil – these are the fundamental forces that most shape our world.

The second theory is exactly the opposite. It essentially says that individuals are irrelevant: that underlying economic forces make us do what we do. If Caesar didn't conquer Western Europe, some other

Roman would have. The Russian Revolution was inevitable, regardless of which Russian led it. A true understanding of history involves looking at the means of production – at who owns stuff, who profits, who gets exploited, and so on. And doing your best to not then fall asleep.

Anyway, there'll be none of that rubbish in this book. And that is because, in it, I propose a *third* theory of history – an entirely new, and perhaps not entirely stupid, hypothesis about why various things might have happened. That theory, in short, is intoxicants. Beers, wine, spirits. Dope, mushrooms. Opium, heroin. Cocaine, speed and so on. What I'm saying is that, ever since *Australopithecus afarensis* came down from the trees and found some fermented fruit lying about on the ground, human beings have been taking things to relax and generally cope with this hell called 'reality'. From presidents and prime ministers, to painters and poets, to sailors, soldiers and scientists, pretty much everyone has, at some time, drunk more than they should or taken something that one should not take.

And it's a custom that can have consequences. In my case, these involve waking up after a party confused and embarrassed, then texting a few dozen apologies.

But other consequences can change the course of our world.

So forget the Great Man Theory of History, folks. I would instead like to give you the Trashed Man (not to mention, lots of not-so-straight women). And, above all, forget about the means of production. This book is about what goes on when humans are not being productive at all.

THIRST-QUENCHERS

Beer, wine & spirits

We all have a bit of a dark side, an evil little voice in the back of our heads. It's a little voice that can lead to some very big and bad things, to serious crimes such as murder and rape. It can lead to cruelty and genocide, to savagery and violence. It has even led some men to invest in lycra.

My own little voice, I am sorry to say, sometimes tells me to try and get my dogs drunk. But I'm not going to do it (I think), because it feels a bit wrong – and in any case, probably won't even work.

To get drunk, you see, you need to be able to actually *metabolise* alcohol, rather than just drink it down. If you can't do that, you'll just feel sick and spew. This ability relies on a complex set of proteins that we humans have, with even-more-complex names such as 'alcohol dehydrogenase enzyme', and one particular version that's called 'ADH4'. The canine versions of these proteins aren't efficient enough for them to get drunk, which is good news for my pets because there are times when that voice is quite loud.

Having said that, human beings aren't entirely alone in their ability to get tipsy. If rotting fruits and vegies are exposed to certain bacteria they eventually become alcoholic, but this fact doesn't stop some animals from eating them – and in fact it might even encourage them. Bohemian waxwing birds, for example, only eat rowan berries late in the winter, when the cooler weather means they've begun to ferment, while pen-tailed tree-shrews like to drink fermented palm nectar for about two hours a night – a drink with the same alcoholic content as beer. Drunk bees are also a thing, believe it or not; after drinking fermented nectar they can have flying accidents.

Still, the list of boozy animals is hardly a long one, and what's odd is that there's only one primate on it: us. All of our cousins – chimps, gorillas, gibbons, orangutans and so on – actually have ADH4, and all the rest of those proteins and enzymes that the budding young alcoholic requires, but tests suggest that they don't really work. Simply put, your average gorilla *can* get drunk if she's given vodka in laboratory conditions, but she'll only get drunk a teensy bit – and then almost immediately start to feel very ill.

So what makes *human* primates so good at drinking? The answer is probably just plenty of practice. At some point in our evolutionary past, the ADH4 that's found in humans somehow became about 40 times better at breaking down ethanol. It's a genetic mutation that seems to have occurred about 10 million years ago – just around the time that climate change shrank the forests of Africa and saw endless grasslands grow up in their place. Fresh hanging fruit slowly became harder to come by, so some species would have had to make do with what they found on the ground.

Chances are, our species was one of them. Ever so slowly our tree-dwelling ancestors ran out of trees to dwell in, and so started to walk on two legs. And ever so slowly, they adapted their diet … and developed the ability to become legless.

And it's an ability that they seemed to enjoy. Evidence of humans deliberately *making* alcohol dates back at least eight thousand years.

How has it affected our behaviour since? Dear reader, it's time to find out.

Early evidence of wine-making

- c. 7000 BCE – Residue found on broken pottery in China included traces of compounds from ancient wines
- c. 6000 BCE – Grape seeds and vine dust uncovered at Gadachrili Gora site in Georgia
- c. 5400 BCE – Wine remnants found on Persian pottery jars in Iran
- c. 4100 BCE – Wine press and formation vat discovered in Armenia
- c. 3150 BCE – Wine residue on clay jars found in the tomb of Scorpion I, one of Egypt's first kings

Early evidence of beer-making

- c. 3500–3100 BCE – Evidence found of Mesopotamian beer manufacturing
- c. 2050 BCE – Mesopotamian tablet found to be an early receipt for 5 Silas (approx. 4.5 litres) of 'the best beer' from brewer Alulu
- c. 1981-1975 BCE – Egyptian funerary model shows an ancient brewery at work
- c. 1800 BCE – Sumerian poem *Hymn to Ninkasi* includes praise to the goddess of beer and a beer recipe

Oldest existing alcohol

- c. 350 – Unopened bottle of wine found in a Roman sarcophagus
- c. 1653 – Rüdesheimer Apostelwein stored in the cellar beneath the town hall of Breman in Germany
- c. 1680s – Hungarian Tokaji wine stored in the Royal Saxon cellars in Dresden
- c. 1787 – Wine made by Chateau Lafite estate, believed to be from Thomas Jefferson's cellar

Popular ingredients for making alcohol

- Africa – millet, maize, cassava
- North America – persimmon, agave
- South America – corn, sweet potatoes
- Asia – rice, wheat, sorghum
- Russia – rye

Nicknames for alcohol

- Grog
- Booze
- Liquid courage
- Hooch
- Juice

Alcohol pros

- Improved mood
- Grandiosity
- Heightened sense of confidence
- May reduce risk of heart disease
- May reduce risk of diabetes

Alcohol cons

- Nausea and vomiting
- Loss of bladder and bowel control
- Blurred vision
- Blackouts
- Temporary loss of consciousness

Alcohol big-time cons

- Death of brain cells
- Liver damage
- Pancreatitis
- Coma
- Death

FROM HUNTERS TO BOOZERS

Did beer kick-start civilisation?

'Alcohol is the anaesthesia by which we endure the operation of life.'

— George Bernard Shaw

The Reformation, the Renaissance, the Industrial Revolution. World War II, Hawthorn's premiership three-peat. There have been many important events in the history of humankind – many moments that have affected us all.

But one event, I'd say, stands alone in its importance, far, far above all the rest – and, no, I'm not talking about Hawthorn's seven straight grand finals in the mid-to-late 1980s. I'm talking about that time in the Middle East about 12,000 years ago, when a bunch of nomadic hunter-gatherers decided to stop nomadically hunting and gathering, and try their hands at some farming instead.

That decision to settle down, clear some trees, dig a hole and grow grain was humanity's biggest move in literally millions of years. It's pretty much on a par with the time some ape-like creature climbed down from a tree, spent some time on the ground and thought, 'Hey, this is better.'

'Why's that?' you ask, understandably puzzled. 'What's so great about grain? I mean, I like fibre as much as the next person, but sure …'

'Here is why,' I swiftly reply, with sincere apologies for cutting you off. It's because farming didn't just lead to more regular bowel motions. It led to what we very loosely call 'civilisation'. Raising animals, growing crops, building shelter, sharing space: these things require a level of cooperation that throwing spears simply didn't entail. Whereas once *homo sapiens* had moved around in tiny little groups, hunting bison, hoarding berries and so forth, all of a sudden, we all became property owners, with all the complicated rules and commitments that property ownership entails. All of a sudden, we started living in large-scale communities with ploughs, wheels and fences – and more to the point, complex customs and laws.

It was the beginning of a journey that led to music, science, philosophy and art, and may well have come to a dead end with the Kardashians.

Anyway, God bless bread, right? Because that's what all this grain was for?

Wrong, say a significant number of archaeologists and botanists. The human race's motive for cultivating nutritious wild grasses may actually have been to make and drink beer. Pretty much every product of civilisation that you can see around you right now – this book, that table, the TV you're about to switch on – could well represent the later stages of a journey that began with the simple desire to get pissed.

It's a theory that's been around for decades, thanks to an American archeologist and anthropologist named Robert Braidwood. 'Could the discovery that a mash of fermented grain yielded a palatable and nutritious beverage have acted as a greater stimulant towards the experimental selection and breeding of the cereals than the discovery of flour and bread-making,' that snappy phrase-maker wondered in the *Scientific American*, way back in 1952.

The short answer is that we simply don't know. While we can be confident that our ancestors started growing grains about 12,000 years ago, evidence relating to *which* grains and *why* is quite literally thin on the ground. But it's worth pointing out that archaeologists recently dug up some beer-brewing troughs in what's now Turkey, and according to carbon-dating they're around 11,000 years old.

It's also worth noting that bread-making would have been a difficult business 12,000 years ago, given the primitive reaping technology that was then available. After collecting tiny return of grain for their labour and carefully removing the chaff, ancient farmers would have then had to spend God-knows-how-long grinding it all into flour, and monitoring some sort of fire-oven, all for the sake of just one little loaf.

Alcohol, in contrast, is comparatively easy to create. For fermentation – the magic that turns grass into booze – to take place all you need is some water and yeast.

So raise a glass to alcohol, I say. Then drink it down, fill it up and drink more. Alcohol may well be the cause of many of society's problems, but without it, we might not have a society at all.

> **DRINKING ETIQUETTE AROUND THE WORLD**
>
> With alcohol came civilisation – and more than one 'civilised' way to drink it. Here are a few to keep in mind next time you head overseas:
>
> - Never clink glasses together when drinking beer (Hungary)
> - Maintain eye contact when toasting (Sweden)
> - Pour and receive your drink with two hands (Korea)
> - Vodka shots should be downed in one (Russia)
> - Never fill a wine glass more than halfway (France)
> - Never top up your own drink – let your host do it (Japan)
> - If you don't finish your drink, pour it back in the bottle (Kazakhstan)
> - Always return a shout (Australia)

DRINK LIKE AN EGYPTIAN

How beer built the Pyramids

'Work is the curse of the drinking classes.'
                                                    Oscar Wilde

One of the wonders of the world, the Pyramids of Giza have been called all sorts of things, from 'powerful', 'spectacular', 'iconic' and 'extraordinary', to the more prosaic 'pyramid-shaped'. Constructed during Egypt's Fourth Dynasty, they were the world's tallest man-made structure for nearly 38 centuries, and have been fascinating tourists for over 45. When Moses was just a slip of a lad, these suckers were already 1000 years old. Some even say they might even be as old as Cher.

But the big question is, who built them? For a long time it seemed the answer was 'slaves', but nowadays we know different. It was actually a paid workforce of sorts. The pyramids were put together by about 20,000 artisans, labourers, foremen and craftsmen over a period of about 20 years.

We also know that they were paid in beer. Recent archaeological excavations in and around the pyramids have uncovered about five square kilometres' worth of long-hidden tombs set aside for more senior stonemasons. In amongst their skeletons, archaeologists have found beer jars and wine vats intended to keep these workers hydrated in the afterlife – and plenty of evidence that they stayed juiced up in this one.

Records show that while the pyramids were being built, beer was dished out three times a day – in the morning, at lunch and at night. 'For the pyramids, each worker got a daily ration of four to five litres,' said the University of Pennsylvania's Dr Patrick McGovern. 'It was a source of nutrition, refreshment and reward for all the hard work. It was beer for pay. You would have had a rebellion on your hands if they'd run out. The pyramids might not have been built if there hadn't been enough beer.'

And Egyptian civilisation itself might have struggled to get off the ground were it not for the sweet amber ale. Made out of boiled water, honey, barley and herbs, and about as thick and sweet as a milkshake, ancient Egyptian beer was safer to drink than the dank old Nile, and a far better source of nutrition. To drink water back then was to drink liquid bacteria; to drink milk was to drink something sour. In a world that was hot, dirty and utterly fridge-less, beer was drunk daily by the entire population, regardless of age, wealth or gender. The hieroglyph for it was even in the word 'meal'.

And in practical terms it meant 'money' as well. Coins being fairly rare for much of Egypt's history, beer helped the wheels of commerce to turn. Public officials and priests were paid in the stuff, and merchants used it as a unit of trade. The standard basic wage was ten loaves of bread and one-third to two full jugs of beer per day.

Guarded over by Osiris, the God of Regeneration, and considered sacred in the temples of Hathor, beer was quite simply 'the national drink' of the land of the Pharaohs.

If you want to walk like an Egyptian, just walk into a pub.

WORKING HARD FOR THE TINNIES

If you thought that the practice of paying for manual labour in beer ended with the Ancient Egyptians, I'd suggest that you think again. A government-funded program in present-day Amsterdam recruits alcoholics to clean the streets and pays them in – yes – beer. The participants spend a few hours picking up rubbish, and in return they receive five cans of beer, half a pouch of rolling tobacco, ten euros and a nice, hot lunch. It might sound a touch counterproductive, but organisers consider the practice a first step towards recovery, insofar as it gives participants a sense of purpose and, well, something to do.

BEWARE OF OVERLY BIG NIGHTS

A big wooden horse will only get you so far

'I envy people who drink. At least they have something to blame everything on.'

Oscar Levant

We don't know whether the *Iliad* is true, but we do know that it is long. Chryseis, Glaucus, Hephaestus, Hermes: these are not skin conditions, or obscure STDs, or some poorly named new brands of swimwear. They are just four in the near-endless cast of characters that populate the oft-retold tale of the Trojan War. Described by Homer in both the *Illiad* and the *Odyssey*, and rebooted by Virgil in yet another epic poem called the *Aeneid*, the ten-year-long conflict between the Greeks and the Trojans too often feels like it's being told in real time.

But eventually, of course, the story *does* actually end, thanks to cunning Odysseus and his big wooden horse. The Greek general came up with the now-famous idea of pretending to retreat, but actually having most of his troops sail a few miles down the coast. The Greeks who remain, of course, build said big wooden horse, leave it on the beach and huddle inside.

Having seen the ships sail away, the Trojan soldiers eventually come out of their fortress, see the horse and decide to drag it back in. But as they all fall asleep that night, a trapdoor opens and ropes drop to the ground. Greek soldiers creep out and quietly unlock the gates. Their comrades rush in and wholesale slaughter ensues. Beware of Greeks bearing gifts, as someone once put it. (Shakespeare, I'd imagine, or someone like that. If you've come here for meticulous referencing you've come to the wrong place.)

What's missing from this summary of the story, however, is the vital role played by booze. We tend to forget that when the Trojan schmucks decided to drag the horse in, they didn't just stand around admiring it for a bit, then yawn, stretch and go get some shut-eye. Some of them were aware that it might be a trick.

For example, the *Aeneid* describes a Trojan called Laocoön who 'rushed down eagerly from the heights of the citadel', to confront them. 'O unhappy citizens, what madness?' he supposedly shouted. 'Do you think the enemy's sailed away? Or do you think any Greek gift's free of treachery? Is that Ulysses' reputation? Either there are Greeks in hiding, concealed by the wood, or it's been built as a machine to use against our walls, or spy on our homes, or fall on the city from above, or it hides some other trick: Trojans, don't trust this horse.'

It's a pity, of course, that this man's name was Laocoön, but I think we can all agree that he made a good point. Nonetheless, 'trust this horse' his compatriots did, and if you've read this book's blurb, you can probably guess why. They'd just won a war and they wanted to get shitfaced; the battle was over, it was time for a drink.

As Homer wrote in *The Odyssey*, 'And so the wooden horse was brought within the City's walls, accompanied with much feasting, drinking and rejoicing by the triumphant and war-weary Trojans throughout the day and into the night as they celebrated their victorious ending of the long Trojan War.'

'The citizens of Troy slept deeply following their raucous celebrations' – and, needless to add, most of them never woke up.

Now someday, dear reader, you might find yourself in a war, and not see much value in a fake farm animal. Just try to remember that if your enemy's pissed, even the silliest of plans might just work.

UNUSUAL HANGOVER CURES

When you've woken up hungover, your city sacked and fields laid to waste, you probably need a bit of a pick-me-up. Here are some of the more exciting suggestions on offer:

- Ground rhino horns (Vietnam)
- Deep-fried canary (Ancient Rome)
- Dried bull penis (Sicily)
- Pickled sheep eyeballs in tomato juice (Mongolia)
- Sparrow droppings in brandy (Hungary)

GREAT AUSTRALIAN PISS-UPS

Sir George Reid, 1903

'Never have I seen such enthusiasm for water – and so little of it drunk.'

Our fourth prime minister discussing the celebrations for the opening of the Kalgoorlie pipeline.

Dawn Fraser, 1964

'We chose a fine big Olympic banner with the five circles on it, and one of my companions bunked himself up on the shoulders of the other. They swayed around a little, and they swore once or twice; but finally they pulled the flag loose. "Quick," said one of them. "Cop this." I took the flag. "Go for your life," said the other. "The [police] are coming."'

In her autobiography Below the Surface, *Dawn Fraser describes a drunken night stealing flags at the Tokyo Olympics.*

Michael Caton, 2015

'I hated seeing the words "Harry finishes his beer" when I had an 8am call. By 11am, after doing several takes, I would be completely shickered, to use a good old Jewish phrase. And I'd still have to finish my work for the day.'

Michael Caton played Harry on The Sullivans *at a time when prop departments didn't believe in fake beer.*

Bernard Tomic, 2012

'So far as I am aware, there's no suggestion Mr Tomic has committed any offence of any kind. If there is, he certainly hasn't been charged or even questioned about it. So I'm really not sure what all the ruckus is about.'

The tennis player's lawyer after his client got into a drunken, half-naked punch-up late at night in a Gold Coast hot tub.

Brendan Fevola, 2009

'I pretty much made a dick of myself that night ... obviously had too much to drink. I don't think I missed too many people that night. I want to express my deep sorriness again.'

Former AFL star Brendan Fevola after a 12-hour bender at the Brownlow Medal count.

St Kilda Football Club, 2013

'He was talking to one of the footballers then another footballer went behind him. He had one of those gas lighters that you light a stove up [with]. He basically opened the flame.

'I saw that his shirt, because we were hired as security, and pants went alight and it slowly started. You know, flames started appearing.'

An observer of the night some St Kilda footballers hired – and allegedly set fire to – a dwarf entertainer.

ALEXANDER THE GREAT ALCOHOLIC

How drunkenness destroyed a great city

'None of the men who in this country have left footprints behind them have been cold water men.'

Sir John Robertson

'When Alexander saw the breadth of his domain, he wept for there were no more worlds to conquer.'

Do you remember that line from *Die Hard*? Well Hans Gruber got it wrong. Actually written by Plutarch, one of those ancient toga-wearing types, the original line said pretty much exactly the opposite: 'Alexander wept for other worlds to conquer'. Personally I'd trust Alan Richman over most ancient essayists.

Regardless, both lines refer to Alexander the Great, the boy-king who conquered half the world by the time he hit 30 without once losing a battle or in any way messing up his great hair. Placed on the throne of Macedonia at the age of 20, after his father popped off in unpleasant circumstances, the blond one used that tiny state's tiny army to unite all of Greece, then headed off east to crush the vast Persian Empire.

Vast empire crushed, he thought, 'Why stop there?' and proceeded to clobber everyone in his path for some 5000 kilometres. When the boy-king popped off himself at age 32, he left behind an empire that stretched from Egypt to India, and a reputation as one of history's great generals.

But it would be unjust to pretend that his achievements certainly didn't end there, for Alex also left behind a reputation as one of history's great alcoholics. A devoted member of the cult of Dionysus (the ancient Greek god of wine), the all-conquering one was fond of all-night booze-ups, and equally committed to quenching his thirst through the day.

Historians such as John O'Brien believe that Alexander's 'escape into alcoholism and desire to conquer the world were two sides of the same coin' – that coin being an 'uncertainty about his own identity, and a desperate desire to prove himself'. Whether or not this is true, it's hard to doubt Allison Weintraub's assertion that 'alcohol played a major role in his decisions, actions, and frame of mind ... As Alexander's use of alcohol amplified, his mood and temperament became progressively more violent and unstable, which caused his companions to fear him ... (and) finally resulted in his demise.'

Want evidence? Well, try visiting the city of Persepolis, the ceremonial capital of the Persian Empire, a glorious mass of gold and marble in what's now southern Iran.

Only you can't, because Alex burned it down. Packed to the gills with priceless art and irreplaceable texts, ornate statues, vast temples and so on, that architectural marvel was reduced to a pile of ash because a 26-year-old got a bit pissed over lunch.

Here's what happened according to Quintus Curtius: after conquering the city in 330 BCE, Alex and his pals 'were feasting, and intoxication was growing as the drinking went on'. 'He took part in prolonged banquets at which women were present ... harlots who were accustomed to live with armed men with more licence than was fitting.'

'One of these, Thais by name, herself also drunken, declared that the king would win most favour among all the Greeks, if he should order the palace of the Persians to be set on fire ... When a drunken strumpet had given her opinion on a matter of such moment, one or two, themselves also loaded with wine, agreed. The king, too, more greedy for wine than able to carry it, cried: "Why do we not, then, avenge Greece and apply torches to the city?"

'All had become heated with wine, and so they arose when drunk to fire the city which they had spared when armed. The king was the first to throw a firebrand upon the palace, then the guests and the servants and courtesans. The palace had been built largely of cedar, which quickly took fire and spread the conflagration widely.'

Good times.

Mind you, being one of Alexander's drinking buddies wasn't always so great – and if you don't believe me, just ask Cleitus the Black. One of the boy-king's oldest friends, Cleitus even saved the Conqueror's life in 334 BCE, when he was cornered at the Battle of the Granicus. But that didn't stop Alex from running him through with a spear when he said something slightly tactless during a drunken dinner.

Equally fun were the 'Drinking Olympics', a competition Alexander organised to celebrate his conquest of India. It involved drinking until you could drink no more. And then, yes, drinking quite a bit more. And then drinking some more after that. It's said that of the 42 drinkers, 35 died immediately after the match. The rest, including the winner who had swallowed 12 litres of wine, died a few days later.

The good news (unless you were a wine merchant) was that not all that long after this, Alex himself all of a sudden died too. He passed away very abruptly at age 32 after coming down with a fever in Babylon. To this day, we still don't know what said 'fever' was – or, indeed, if it was a fever at all. But we *do* know that he came down with it right after two straight days of 'drinking far into the night'.

And we also know that he kept on drinking while he was ill. For Professor John O'Brien, the hot, sweaty and dehydrated king's 'insistence on wine – rather than water, [to slake his thirst] only makes sense if the "fever" was an acute case of alcohol withdrawal'. No ancient army could kill the Great One, or slow his Empire's remorseless tread. But a few fermented grapes seem to have stopped him right in his tracks, and in so doing, changed the world.

THE REAL AUSSIE THIRST-QUENCHER

Australians may have more in common with Alexander the Great than we realise – at least when it comes to our favourite drink. While we're known as a nation of beer-guzzlers, studies have shown that Australia's *actual* favourite drink is red wine, the tipple of choice for 27 per cent of Aussie drinkers. Beer comes second at 24 per cent, followed by white wine at 16 per cent, and finally cider and whiskey both at 7 per cent. And in surprising news for people with tastebuds, no less than 3 per cent of us apparently prefer to drink rum. I myself would probably rather drink petrol.

THAT SINKING FEELING

How a boozy party boat brought on a war

'He that drinks fast, pays slow.'

Benjamin Franklin

If Prince Charles suddenly died it'd be sad and all, but succession-wise, not such a problem. This is because Prince William is waiting right there in the wings, all ready to step up and take his place on the throne.

And even if *he* happened to die too, in some tragic royal massacre involving terrorism or some unusually fierce corgis, there'd be no need to worry, because we'd still have that plump little cherub Prince George standing by, all ready to grasp the crown, orb and sceptre. Australians may object to this family on all sorts of levels – they're anachronisms, they're fox hunters, they're inbred, they're bald – but there's no denying that it's full of legitimate heirs, every single one of them potentially entitled to rule.

But when King Henry I died in 1135, I'm sorry to say that things were a little more complicated. Close observers could tell this by way his death sparked a vicious civil war.

How? Well, the problem was that while Henry was an enthusiastic pants man, and had pumped out at least a dozen kids during the course of his reign, only two of said kids were made with his lawful wedded wife and, as such, entitled to rule.

Complicating matters further was the fact that by the time Henry died, the only legitimate boy, William, was dead. The only legitimate girl, Matilda, had an even more serious problem, that being that she was a girl.

So when Henry popped off leaving Matilda to rule, a few right-thinking lords naturally responded, 'No way.' Not caring for this newfangled political-correctness-gone-mad, they swung their support behind one Stephen of Blois, Matilda's penis-owning cousin from France. A battle or two later, he was wearing the crown.

But he never wore it very comfortably. The 19 years of Stephen's reign is known amongst historians as 'The Anarchy': a two-decade long orgy of bloodshed, chiefly characterised by theft, riot and rape. It was a period of lawlessness, poverty and constant pitched battles. A period in which England's nobles switched their support back and forth between the two warring cousins, and the peasants who fought for them went to cold, early graves.

'I have neither the ability nor the power to tell all the horrors nor all the torments they inflicted upon wretched people in this country,' said one observer, before deciding to give it a bash anyway. The rival cousins 'levied taxes on the villages every so often, and called it "protection money". When the wretched people had no more to give, they robbed and burned the villages so that you could easily go a whole day's journey and never find anyone occupying a village, nor land tilled. Then corn was dear, and meat and butter and cheese, because there was none in the country. Wretched people died of starvation; some lived by begging for alms, who had once been rich men; some fled the country.

'There had never been till then greater misery in the country, nor had heathens ever done worse than they did.'

Bad, very bad. Grim stuff, indeed. And what makes it even worse was that it was entirely avoidable. While we can't in total fairness blame Henry I's daughter, Matilda, for being a woman, we *can* blame his son for being dead. Chockful of chest hair and XY chromosomes, and with what was then called a 'spindle' swinging between his two legs, Prince William would have been a perfectly acceptable heir to all those less-than-feminist dukes, knights and earls. Had *he* been around to take hold of the crown, there would have been no civil war, and plenty of corn, cheese and butter for all.

But no, he was dead. Deceased. Gone. Six feet under. Insensate. And the reason for this was that he liked a drink.

In 1120, you see, William and his father had been in France for some reason, and so had to make their way back to England across the Channel. The original idea had been for them to take the same boat, but that plan changed at the final moment, during a 'prodigious feast' in Barfleur.

One Thomas FitzStephen, the young owner of a new and super-fast ship, appeared at the King's table with the news that the luxurious 'White Ship' would soon be in harbour, and would be available to escort His Majesty home. Henry was in a hurry, and so declined the kind offer. But he told his teenage son that he could stick around until nightfall if he liked and then take this new ship instead.

So stick around until nightfall the Prince and his pals did – and, while they were at it, they got into the piss. They also shared several barrels of wine with the crew, and arranged for many more to be taken on board.

When it finally came time to stagger on board themselves, it seems that these youths were so drunk that they decided that there was still time to overtake the king's ship. So William ordered the equally intoxicated crew to go full steam ahead. 'As the drunken oarsmen were rowing with all their might, and the luckless helmsman paid scant attention to steering the ship through the sea, the port side of the White Ship struck violently against a huge rock, which was uncovered each day as the tide ebbed and covered once more at high tide. Two planks were shattered and, terrible to relate, the ship capsized without warning.'

William and 300 nobles capsized along with it. Fifteen years later, Henry I died and the nation was plunged into anarchy.

A TROUGH OF BLOOD

How alcohol helped save Europe

> *'Better sleep with a sober cannibal than a drunken Christian.'*
>
> — Herman Melville

The greatest pleasure is to vanquish your enemies and chase them before you, to rob them of their wealth and see those dear to them bathed in tears, to ride their horses and clasp to your bosom their wives and daughters.

Not my words, I hasten to add. They were said by one Genghis Khan.

Far and away history's greatest general, and almost certainly its most active rapist, that Mongol warlord conquered nearly 12 million square miles in 25 short years, from the east coast of China all the way to Kiev. Not what you'd call an especially nice man, Genghis insisted on being presented with virgins by every territory he took, and often tortured said virgins' brothers and dads.

And the nasty vibes certainly didn't stop there. As the historian David Nicolle notes, 'terror and mass extermination of anyone opposing them was a well-tested Mongol tactic.' If you surrendered to Genghis there was a small chance he'd kill you, but if you didn't, it was a stone-cold certainty. He's said to have exterminated over a million people – the inhabitants of an entire Persian city – after one of them hit his son-in-law with an arrow. And he's thought to have had another 1.3 million citizens slaughtered in what's now Turkmenistan because their Sultan had somehow given him the shits. 'Each soldier in the army was allotted around 300 people to kill. Most had their throats slit. Others were led out, 20 at a time, to be drowned in a trough of blood,' Nicolle notes.

All in all, the Great Khan's hijinks are thought to have killed around 40 million people. That's about a tenth of the entire world at the time.

The secret of his success, should you be interested, is in fact not a secret at all. Unlike just about every other 13th-century army in Asia and Europe, Genghis's soldiers did their soldiering on horseback. A nomadic people who didn't really do houses or farms, the Mongol tribes were literally raised in the saddle, and learned how to ride and shoot little birds almost before they could walk.

For thousands of years before Genghis got slaughtering, the Mongols had been content to just slaughter each other – and they had done so in a wholly unique way. This is to say that, rather than faffing about with armour and lances and swords and clubs, they would simply ride up to within 500 metres of an enemy, shoot him right in the face, and then quickly ride off out of range. Then they would turn around, ride back, shoot one of his colleagues, dash off and do it all over again. Sounds simple in theory, but in practice it isn't, and other armies struggle to respond effectively to the speed of the Mongol attacks and retreats.

So when Genghis united the warring Mongol tribes into a single army, the result was an army that was essentially invincible. Under his leadership, in the words of one monk, 'an immense horde of that detestable race of Satan burst from their mountain-bound regions, and ... rushed forth like demons'.

As Europeans watched the horde's remorseless march west from what's now China, it seemed like the long-prophesied reign of the Antichrist was very near at hand. When it came to overall population and military technology, the combined kingdoms of medieval Europe would have been no match for China's state-of-the-art, two-million-soldier-strong armies, and *those* armies had been no match for the Khan.

But just as all good things come to an end, bad things occasionally do too. In 1227, Genghis Khan died from unknown causes, in what must have been a pleasing development for pretty much everyone who'd met him – not least the 500-odd former virgins forced to spend life as his concubines. But you'll be glad to know that his spirit of conquest lived on, and his 'Devil's Horsemen' remained as hideous as ever.

Under the new Khan, Ögedei – Genghis's loveable scamp of a son – the hordes of Satan continued their satanic march west, laying waste to Russia and the Ukraine. In 1240 they arrived in Eastern Europe and promptly celebrated by slaughtering about a million

Hungarians, then crushing a combined force of Germans and Poles.

The whole of the continent now lay at their mercy. Western civilisation, Christendom, call it what you will: it was all about to come to an end.

Only it didn't; Europe's still here. Which, if we overlook the French, is an excellent thing.

How? Why? When? I'll tell you. It's because one day, unprompted, and entirely out of nowhere, the satanic hordes suddenly decided to turn back. Just like that, they packed up their tents, hopped on their horses and galloped off east, leaving Europe behind forever. Western civilisation, Christendom, call it what you will: the whole damn package was miraculously saved.

God, naturally enough, got the credit for all this, but I think we all know that the real hero was alcohol. While Europe's rain probably helped put its potential conquerors off (boggy fields aren't all that much fun for horses), the main reason for their abrupt about-turn was the sudden death of the 55-year-old Ogedai. Electing a new Khan was a complicated business, and long-distance ballots were in no way an option. Representatives of all the different tribes had to gather for a vote in Mongolia, and so conquering Christendom had to be put on hold. That's what's known as a welcome death.

But how did Ogedai die, I hear you ask? The answer is alcohol. Sweet, blessed alcohol. A serious, long-time boozer, this less-great Khan had a cup that specially designed to hold over three pints, and servants whose sole job was to keep it topped up.

And it's fair to say that they did their job well. He collapsed abruptly one dawn after an all-night drinking binge – the new 'Antichrist' dying, rather like the regular Christ, in order that we all might live.

> **RUSSIANS DO IT BETTER**
>
> While power relations in Eurasia have shifted over the centuries, its residents' taste for alcohol remains much the same. When the World Health Organization conducted a study on which countries consume the most alcohol, the top 10 nations were all in Eastern Europe, with Belarus taking top spot. On average each Belarusian consumes 17.5 litres of alcohol per year, double what experts consider dangerous. Russia came in at number four, a statistic that is perhaps unsurprising when you consider that beer was not even classified as alcohol there until 2013.

SELIM THE DRUNKARD

How fine wine started a war

'Beer is made by men, wine by God.'

Martin Luther

There are many silly reasons to start a war, as George W Bush well knows. You might remember that that president invaded Iraq because he knew for a *fact* that it was hiding weapons of mass destruction, despite the UN's failure to find anything of the sort. It turned out that this fact was actually complete fiction, which must have been a touch annoying for the tens of thousands who died.

But, hey, we all make mistakes (as Aussies voters say to themselves whenever Mr Turnbull appears on the telly). Us still-alive people should just move on from Iraq – I'm pretty sure George has.

And in any case, even imaginary weapons of mass destruction may well be a better reason to invade a foreign country than the mere fact that it grows some good wine. But such seems to have been what prompted an Ottoman sultan called Selim the Drunkard to conquer Cyprus back in 1571.

Also known as Selim the Sot – or in more formal circles, Selim II – the Drunkard was a short, fat, and lazy youngest son who, as such, was never supposed to end up a sultan. He thus never received the basic grounding in governance and soldiering that was customary for all heirs to the throne. Stuck in a palace, surrounded by servants, and with his very own fully stocked harem, this princeling instead spent his teenage years becoming 'addicted to sexual and alcoholic pleasures'. He basically lived the life of Hugh Hefner, only with more head jobs and a great deal less editing.

But all that changed when Selim's father, Suleiman the Magnificent, suddenly fell out with his two eldest sons. Naturally that meant having both of them strangled – a decision that started to seem a bit hasty when the third-oldest brother then caught smallpox and died.

All of a sudden the fourth-oldest brother was first in line to the throne (rather than just first in line to the bar). And when his Magnificent dad died in 1566, this pot-bellied alcoholic found himself in charge of no less than 25 million people – the head of an empire that stretched from south-eastern Europe all the way to the Persian Gulf. Selim was the Sultan of Sultans and the Khan of the Khans, the Commander of the Faithful and Successor of the Prophet.

But don't worry, it didn't interfere with his lifestyle. In what's considered by historians to be the start of the Ottoman Empire's long, slow decline, the indolent Selim was happy to let government more or less ground to a halt while he kept busy enjoying drunk orgies.

But perhaps this is a little unfair. The Sot *did* take an interest in his Empire on one occasion, after all, after he took a liking to a certain fine wine. 'At some banquet, where the wine of Cyprus flowed in abundance,' wrote historian Joseph von Hammer-Purgstall, a courtier suggested that it would be an easy thing for the Sultan 'to render himself master of the native country of this noblest of wines', which at the time was controlled by Venice.

'Good idea,' thought the Commander of the Faithful, and so he commanded 300 ships to sail forth.

Unfortunately, it turned out that rendering himself master of Cyprus was *not* actually that easy. Around 30,000 people all had to die first. Selim lost around 90 per cent of his navy at the hands of the Holy League, a combined armada of ships from Venice, Genoa and Spain. It was Europe's largest naval battle in over 1000 years, its first major victory against the Ottoman Empire and the end point of Ottoman expansion. History was changed forever and 'the sea was red with blood'.

But on the upside, Selim got his wine. And he got to enjoy it for four glorious years until, drunk, hot and wet, he managed to fall over and break his skull on the marble floor of a Turkish bathhouse.

THE WORLD'S MOST EXPENSIVE WINES

There aren't many wines that would cost an entire empire, but these bottles might come close:

- Chateau Margaux, 1787 (US$500,000 for 750ml)
- Screaming Eagle Cabernet Sauvignon, 1992 (US$500,000 for 750ml)
- Chateau Lafite, 1787 (US$160,000 for 750ml)
- Penfolds Grange Hermitage, 1951 (US$38,420 for 750ml)
- Cheval Blanc, 1947 (US$33,781 for 750ml)

THE BRITS GO ABROAD

The invasion that was foiled by fine wine

'Let us have wine and women, mirth and laughter, sermons and soda water the day after.'

Lord Byron

The problem with England, as has often been noted, is that it's so full of English people. Wonderful folk in moderation, of course, with all those nice puddings and period dramas. But taken in their millions, the effect is quite grim – the country's not so much *Pride and Prejudice* as an especially bleak episode of *The Office*.

So I suppose we can all thank our lucky stars that this Englishness is not also a problem with Spain. Or rather, we can thank alcohol.

In 1625, you see, His Most Gracious Majesty Charles I officially sanctioned the invasion of Spain. The English king's plan was to take hold of the port of Cadiz, and from there start to conquer the coast.

With a bit of luck, his troops would also be able to snatch the Spanish treasure fleet when it returned from the mines of South America laden with silver and gold.

Apart from the fact that said fleet had actually already returned, things went pretty much according to plan ... or at least they did right up until the moment the English arrived in Cadiz. Since the local Spanish soldiers had abandoned the town in order to await reinforcements elsewhere, the 100 or so English ships all docked in good order – but the same thing couldn't be said for the English supplies. It turned out that nobody had really thought to pack any.

It was not the sort of oversight that you'd expect from a battle-hardened commander like Sir Edward Cecil. Or rather, it wasn't until you realised that each of his battles to date had been fought not with ships, but on land.

Anyway, not to worry. What sort of wusses need water and food? Anxious to head off an approaching Spanish force (which, as it turned out, was not approaching at all), Cecil quickly marched his 8000 drink-free men through several dozen miles of dry, salty marshland underneath the heat of a blazing sun. By nightfall they still had not seen the enemy, and even worse, they had not seen a river.

Anyway, not to worry, there must be food and water somewhere. All they had to do was forage. And so forage the foreign invaders did ... until some of them discovered a deserted building, which happened to be the wine store for an entire Spanish fleet. Dry of mouth, empty of stomach and perhaps just a touch overheated of brain, the soldiers 'were permitted to fill themselves so much with the wine they found in the cellars and other places they plundered, that they became more like beasts than men'.

And that, in case you're wondering, was not a good thing. The 8000 English beasts immediately proceeded to 'run riot', menacing the officers, shooting each another and breaking into another wine store when Cecil ordered it locked. 'No words of exhortation, no blows of correction would restrain them,' a senior officer later reported. They broke into the wine rooms shouting that they fought for King Charles and could take whatever they wanted.

In the morning, however, they were more like *hungover* wretches – and this in an age when Berocca was not yet invented. The soldiers were *so* hungover, in fact, that any further soldiering was out of the question. There was no way that anyone could march inland into battle. And there was also no way that any of them could safely stay put, since that meant building a fort. In fact, even finding the strength to carry a weapon was a difficult, nay unreasonable, ask. So when a despairing Cecil surrendered to the inevitable and ordered a retreat to the ships, many soldiers simply abandoned their weapons. They also left behind at least 1000 of their Aspirin-less comrades who were just too hungover to move. Most of them had their throat cuts by Spanish soldiers later that day, which at least meant an end to their headaches.

So Spain thus remains the home of the Spanish. Though with all the lager-swilling package tourists slowly colonising the Costa del Sol, Charles's grand vision of an English Iberia may sadly still have some legs.

IRISH PHRASES MEANING 'HUNGOVER'

Nobody describes drinking (and all the related pros and cons) quite like the Irish, so here are a few choice Irish ways to describe a hangover that could certainly have been applied to the British army in Spain.

- 'Brown bottle flu'
- 'In rag order'
- 'In lego'
- 'Mouth like a fur boot'
- 'Puking your ring'

A PURITANICAL PISS-UP

How a beer shortage helped shape America

'If God had intended us to drink beer, he would have given us stomachs.'

David Daye

If you're prepared to overlook thousands of years of Native American culture (and let's face it, people generally are), US history essentially began with a ship called the *Mayflower*, which set sail from England in the year 1620.

Aboard the *Mayflower* were 100 or so hardy Pilgrims – various fanatically religious types who, unhappy with the all-powerful Church of England, had been granted permission by King James I to be unhappy elsewhere. His Charter of Virginia granted them land rights in an area that was then called Virginia for the purposes of 'propagating of Christian Religion to such People as yet live in Darkness and miserable

Ignorance of the true Knowledge and Worship of God, and may in time bring the Infidels and Savages living in those parts to human Civility'. (Or in other words, 'Go bother the Indians if you must. Please just leave the rest of us alone.')

But while Puritans were best avoided at parties, it would be wrong to imagine that they were particularly pure. 'One of the things we understand now is that the initial ship that came over from England to Massachusetts Bay actually carried more beer than water,' said the historian Bruce Bustard.

But apparently even *that* much beer still wasn't quite enough. The *Mayflower* never actually made it to Virginia, as per the conditions of their charter, but instead landed about 800 miles north of where they were supposed to, at a place in Cape Cod that they called Plymouth Rock.

And the reason for this was that they were running out of beer.

'We could not now take time for further search and consideration, our victuals being much spent, especially our beer,' is how one Puritan would later explain the last-minute change of plan. Since the ship's crew wanted some beer left over for the long journey home, their God-bothering passengers 'were hastened ashore and made to drink water'.

And while they didn't actually eat pumpkin pies, as tradition now has it, during that very first Thanksgiving dinner, you'll be glad to know that the Puritans had still put enough in their suitcases to wash it all down with brandy and gin. And while Cape Cod was 'wintry, unsettled and inhospitable', its soil was still good enough to grow carrots, tomatoes, onions, beets, celery, squash, dandelions, and goldenrod – fruits and vegetables which they soon turned into strengthening spirits.

But settling a new continent was a serious business: life wasn't all about dandelion gin. The 120 'first' Americans needed to set up some system of government, and this is where the true significance of the beer shortage kicks in. James I's Charter of Virginia had already set out just such a system, of course – but, technically speaking, the settlers weren't in Virginia. An argument could be made that Cape Cod was outside his formal jurisdiction, and that his Charter's rules and regulations therefore didn't apply.

And make that argument many duly did. Several of the more independent-minded settlers started to cause trouble with 'discontented and mutinous speeches'. No man had the 'power to command them', they insisted (while draining some sort of beetroot-based spirit that could've killed a small mule).

Long and boring speeches like this can have an effect. After people have heard them five or six times, they'll do just about anything to avoid hearing a seventh.

Therefore, the settlers agreed to get together and decide on a new system of government. Written and signed by every single male Puritan – the corridors of power being no place for chicks – the Mayflower Compact of 1620 has been called the foundation stone of American democracy. And it's a system that's democratic to a fault. In America, pretty much *every* public official needs to be elected by the people – and I'm not just talking about senators and members of congress. If you want to be a circuit judge in the States, or on a school board, or a chief of police, or a district attorney, you need to get out there and press the flesh, shake hands, and kiss lots of babies. The number of elected officials reaches over half a million. It's an unbelievably inefficient, expensive and slow-moving system.

And it's a system that essentially began with the principle established in the Mayflower Compact. The principle that every single settler must have his ~~or her~~ say. 'From its crude beginning in Plymouth,' according to the website of the Constitutional Rights Foundation, 'self-government evolved into the town meetings of New England and larger local governments in colonial America. By the time of the Constitutional Convention, the Mayflower Compact had been nearly forgotten, but the powerful idea of self-government had not. Born out of necessity on the *Mayflower*, the Compact made a significant contribution to the creation of a new democratic nation.'

And that contribution all began with beer.

HOW TO TOAST AROUND THE WORLD

Every new charter deserves a new toast, so here are some options you might like to consider the next time you found a new nation.

- *Fill de puta qui no se l'acabi*: 'Whoever doesn't finish their glass is a son of a whore.' (Spain)
- *Bunden i vejret eller resten i håret*: 'Bottoms up or the rest in your hair.' (Denmark)
- *Hau weg die schiesse*: 'Away with that shit.' (Germany)
- *Sláinte bradán bod mór agus bás in Eireann*: 'To having the health of a salmon, a large penis, and a death in Ireland.' (Ireland)
- *Ikkinomi*: 'Drink it in one breath.' (Japan)

HOW TO SAY 'CHEERS' AROUND THE WORLD

- *Na zdravi!* (Czech)
- *Oogy wawa!* (Zulu)
- *Kampai!* (Japanese)
- *Salute!* (Italian)
- *Noroc!* (Romanian)

DUTCH COURAGE

How alcohol has (mostly) helped soldiers

> 'Wine gives courage and makes men more apt for passion.'
>
> — Ovid

'You will never do anything in this world without courage,' said Aristotle.

But if you don't have any courage, there's no need to despair. Buy a bottle of something, slam it all down, and the world is your oyster, to do with as you wish – at least until you need to take a pill and lie down.

I'm talking about 'Dutch courage', of course. It's a term that dates back to the Thirty Years War, a 17th-century conflict between Europe's Catholics and Protestants that ended up killing about eight million people. And quite a few of them, it would seem, were quite pissed. The Dutch soldiers, in particular, liked to drink up before a battle – and when their English allies saw this, they soon followed suit. Gin became an everyday staple in the trenches, warming stomachs, fortifying nerves and generally helping folks fight, kill and die.

But while Dutch courage was certainly a good idea, you could hardly call it a particularly new one. Drinking before battle has been going on forever. Spirits were a daily ration in the Roman army, for example, while ancient Greek soldiers were given wine mixed with water. When Hannibal defeated Rome, he did it with drunk war elephants. And while the Knights Templar may have sworn off sex, most of them remained deeply committed to booze. The phrase 'to drink like a Templar' was a common one in the Middle Ages.

And 'drink like a Templar' is also what most soldiers did during the four-year-long US Civil War. 'No one evil agent so much obstructs this army as the degrading vice of drunkenness,' complained one Confederate general – though over in Europe, generals were more well-disposed. English troops were issued four litres of beer a day during the war against Napoleon, while their French rivals received almost as much wine.

Over in Japan, on the other hand, Samurai warriors didn't so much drink like a Templar, as drink like a Samurai warrior. This involved lots of sake before every battle. Centuries later, Kamikaze pilots got stuck into the rice wine as well, before loading their planes up with bombs and flying them straight into ships.

And as far as the Russian writer Viktor Yerofeyev is concerned, 'the daily ration of vodka given to Russian soldiers in World War II was as important as katyusha rocket launchers in the victory over Nazism'.

But all things in moderation, I say, lest Dutch courage become Dutch craziness. While a drink or two can tune you up nicely for battle, a drink or *ten* can go terribly wrong. History's most famous illustration of this dictum may well be a battle that took place one evening in 1788 between the Austrian army and the ... um ... Austrian army.

According to legend, at least, what happened was this. A year or so into a long war against the Ottoman Empire, 100,000 Austrian troops found themselves in Karansebes, a tiny village in what's now Romania. Having decided to set up camp for the night, they sent out some scouts to survey the area in case some Turkish soldiers were massed somewhere nearby.

They weren't, as it happened, but a few gypsies were. And it turned out they had brandy to sell. The scouts accordingly brought back a few barrels to share with their buddies, but there just wasn't quite enough to go around.

What would you do in this situation? I think the answer is obvious. Very clearly, you would go start a brawl. But – it being dark, and, you know, enemy territory – it turned out that an all-in brawl wasn't a great idea. When the fighting inevitably caused some soldiers to start shooting, a handful of soldiers from further away naturally thought that the Turks had attacked.

Panicking, many of them started to flee across a bridge, in a confused retreat that looked a lot like a charge. Or at least, that's what it looked like to the thousands of also-panicking soldiers on the other side of the bridge, with the result that they got out their guns too.

And things weren't really helped by the fact that the Austrian army was polylingual, a multicultural melting pot of Slavs, Czechs, Hungarians and Poles. According to some accounts, soldiers' screams of 'Halt! Halt!' were misinterpreted as 'Allah! Allah!' by the non-German speaking Slavs.

By morning, some 10,000 Austrian soldiers were dead, and many of the others had a deadly hangover.

GREAT AUSTRALIAN PISS-UPS

Mike Willesee, 1989

'I was sick, and I hadn't worked for a while, when [the producers of *A Current Affair*] called me up and asked if I would host. So I went to the doctor and explained I wasn't feeling right.

'Well he must have thought I was nervous or something so he prescribed Valium. I had never taken Valium. So I took one of those and I still didn't feel right. So I had a scotch. Then I still wasn't feeling right so I had another Valium and another scotch. By the time I got into the studio I was flying.

'When the autocue started rolling, I couldn't read a thing. I was so away with the pixies I started laughing. Look, I didn't abuse anyone. And I didn't fall over, so it could've been worse.'

TV journalist Mike Willesee after appearing slightly worse for wear on A Current Affair.

Glen Milne, 2006

'Please accept this release as an apology to my esteemed colleagues, friends and family for the hurt and embarrassment caused by my actions at the Walkley Awards in Melbourne.

'I was very proud to represent News Ltd as a finalist and was honoured to have been invited to take part in this prestigious event. However, I lamentably mixed alcohol and migraine medication with shocking consequences.

'I apologise too to Stephen Mayne and the organisers of the awards. There is no excuse for my behaviour.'

Glen Milne after stumbling onstage at the Walkley Awards to punch on with fellow journo, Stephen Mayne.

Karl Stefanovic, 2009

'It wasn't any different to any other year – we all get smashed at the Logies and go to work the next day; we'd done it for years and years. But this was the first Logies when stuff really started working on the internet.

'I remember seeing it on *Today Tonight* and going "Oh god". I really was drunk, or at least I certainly looked and sounded drunk.

'I was worried about it initially, but I think it broke down a barrier for me. It's that age-old theory in TV that if you haven't harmed anyone, the public might find it funny. The public have been tremendously supportive – the only drama is that every time I go out now, everybody wants me to get drunk with them.

'For me to look back on it, it's quite funny now.'

The host of the Today Show, *Karl Stefanovic, after a big night at the Logies.*

OI, OI, OI

Is the Australian accent due to hard drinking?

> *'It was lamentable to behold the excess to which drunkenness was carried ... It was no uncommon experience for men to sit round a bucket of spirits and drink it with quart pots until they were unable to stir from the spot.'*
>
> A visitor to Sydney in 1802

Whether or not Australians are an energetic people, it's probably fair to say that our accent is not. Described by some as a 'lazy drawl', and by Winston Churchill as 'the most brutal maltreatment that has ever been inflicted on the mother-tongue of the great English-speaking nations', the Aussie accent involves minimal tongue movement – it's basically one step removed from a mumble. Diphthongs aren't really a thing we do well, and we're also not crash hot with consonants.

So where, exactly, do these strange sounds come from? Where should we point the finger of blame?

The short answer is that nobody really knows, since tape recorders weren't around in convict times. It's clearly a mixture of different, mostly working-class English accents from back in the day, Cockney probably preeminent among them. And (convicts and early settlers being from all over the UK), there's obviously some Scottish, Irish and Welsh accents in there as well. But it's hard to work out what the precise recipe was, since we don't really know what each ingredient sounded like.

But according to Victoria University's Dean Frenkel, there may be one ingredient that we can all still taste. 'The Australian alphabet cocktail was spiked by alcohol,' he recently announced in *The Age*. 'Our forefathers regularly got drunk together, and through their frequent interactions unknowingly added an alcoholic slur to our national speech patterns. For the past two centuries, from generation to generation, drunken Aussie-speak continues to be taught by sober parents to their children.'

In an article that the UK tabloids picked up, and will probably continue to reference until the End of Time, this self-described 'communications expert' insisted that 'the average Australian speaks to just two-thirds capacity, with one third of our articulator muscles always sedentary, as if lying on the couch'.

And just in case this didn't offend you enough, the centuries-old fondness for alcohol 'may also be a contributor to Australia's lack of cultural substance'.

Fortunately, other language experts, like Aidan Wilson, tend to reject this theory 'completely and without reservation'. 'To cause sound changes in a language,' Wilson argues, 'you need to be affecting the way you talk at every moment of every day. I personally find it laughable that Frenkel thinks that there was a critical mass of constantly drunk people – new mothers included – that would enable children to essentially learn inebriated English.'

On that reassuring note, let me leave you with this less-than-reassuring quote. 'They are not a nation of snobs like the English or of extravagant boasters like the Americans or of reckless profligates like the French,' observed writer Marcus Clarke of Australians.

'They are simply a nation of drunkards.'

HOW TO SPEAK WITH AUSTRALIAN ACCENT

Still not convinced that we speak like drunks? Have a look at these snippets of advice for American actors on how to best imitate an Aussie.

'Chew your words before you say them. Aussies don't enunciate like Americans do. When Australians talk, it seems that they don't open their mouths very much and words just blend together.' - *capaworld.capa.org*

'Try not to move your tongue so much. One vocal coach suggests you imagine your tongue laying over an exercise ball.' - *wikihow.com*

'Aussies replace the hard T sound with a short, almost guttural noise instead of a full "tuh" sound.' - *wikihow.com*

'End sentences with an upward intonation. Make every comment sound like a question.' - *peopleof.oureverydaylife.com*

THE UNITED STATES OF ALCOHOL

How the War of Independence was waged over rum

'Beer is proof that God loves us and wants us to be happy.'

— Benjamin Franklin

Most Americans don't know much about Australia, beyond the fact that we all wear akubras, barbecue shrimps and own pet kangaroos. They could probably find us on a map, given time, if said map was carefully labelled. And they're aware, more or less, that we are the home of Hugh Jackman (as well as, alas, Russell Crowe).

But that's about it, really, and that's perfectly fine – because most Americans also don't know much about America. Yankee Doodles see themselves as a beacon of liberty, as the land of the free and the home of the brave. It's a self-image forged during the American Revolution, and since reinforced by a hundred shit action movies. The honest colonials, it's always said, had just had it up to here with Bad King George III, that unelected tyrant with his English troops and big pesky taxes. So those hardy sons of the soil went and stuck it to the man, striking a blow for justice and freedom that still rings around the world to this day.

It's a stirring tale that's actually true, in parts, so long as you overlook the fact that most of these freedom fighters owned a whole heap of slaves. Life, liberty and the pursuit of happiness were only for white folks. And the right to vote was strictly reserved for Protestants – or rather, Protestants who owned land and had a penis. The Declaration of Independence may well have created 'government of, for and by the people', but the people that its creators had in mind weren't necessarily you or your friends.

Also forgotten by today's flag-waving patriots is the big part played in all this by booze. The American Revolution famously kicked off with an incident known as the Boston Tea Party – but tea certainly wasn't the sole drink involved.

Let's go back to Bad King George. In 1773, the monarch was in need of more money, and so decided to impose a big new tax on tea. It was yet another case of this 'taxation without representation' that had for so long given colonials the shits. In Boston, a small group called 'The Sons of Liberty' decided that they could take said shit no more. So they snuck into Boston Harbour and onto some English cargo ships, every single one of them chock full of tea. Then they grabbed 350 crates, threw them all overboard, and – point made – marched off waving a flag.

Mother England responded to the 'Boston Tea Party' with some pretty severe sanctions – sanctions which soon resulted in an all-out war.

Or, at least, so goes the story. The truth of the matter is that King George *hadn't* increased the tax on tea at all. In fact, he had recently lowered it. It was actually London's decision to tax *molasses*, the key ingredient in rum, that got the Sons of Liberty so up in arms. The only reason that they hoed into crates of tea was that there didn't happen to be any molasses on board the ship.

'The idea of "no taxation without representation" originated with molasses and sugar,' said historian Tom Standage. 'When the British tried to tax molasses it struck at the heart of the economy.'

Also, the liver of the economy. Modern-day Americans don't drink very much (though God knows, I would if I had to live there). But things were very different back in the day. The colonies had more pubs per capita than any other business on the continent – and from breakfast through to, well, breakfast, they all tended to be pretty full. According to historian Kristen Burton, the average American used to get through about six gallons of pure alcohol per year, more than three times as much as the average American today. 'Rum was the real spirit of 1776.'

And it's worth noting that rum wasn't just on the Boston Tea Partiers' *minds*; it was also sloshing about in their stomachs. Before deciding that it would be a bright idea to board the British ships, and so spark a war, the 50 or so Sons of Liberty had spent the entire afternoon and evening at a pub, drinking lots of rum, wine and whiskey. It wasn't until quite late in the night that they became 'drunk enough to change history'.

Rum also came in handy during the Revolution itself, when it kicked off a couple of years later with Paul Revere's midnight ride. If you are unfamiliar with the story, allow me to bore you: Revere was a silversmith who rode through the colony of Massachusetts bellowing, 'the British are coming!' to warn his fellow revolutionaries that, well, the British were coming. King George had sent troops to round up some key agitators, but thanks to Revere they were able to slip away, and so go and agitate elsewhere. Henry Wadsworth Longfellow later wrote a famous poem about Revere, but he didn't mention one key point. While it was true that 'through the gloom and the light, the fate of a nation was riding that night', it was riding with a man who was probably sloshed. Revere stopped at a rum distillery halfway through his all-night journey and 'took refreshments' for the best part of an hour.

The leader of the Revolutionary forces, General George Washington, also liked his men cheered and refreshed. 'The benefits arising from moderate use of Liquor, have been experienced in All Armies, and are not to be disputed!' the man who eventually became president declared. 'There should always be a sufficient quantity of spirits with the army, to furnish moderate supplies to the troops ... when they are marching in hot or cold weather, in camp ... or in working parties.'

A sufficient quantity of spirits was also available when Thomas Jefferson wrote the Declaration of Independence over drinks in a Philadelphia tavern. And it's worth noting that the 'Founding Fathers' who went on to sign it included a distiller, a cider maker and a cooper, plus several brewers and a number of rum-smugglers. Jefferson himself was a winemaker of note, while Washington was a part-time whiskey-maker (not to mention a major grower of hemp). One of Benjamin Franklin's great contributions to scholarship, meanwhile, was an essay on why different wines tend to produce different farts.

The record should also show that, just two days before the Founding Fathers signed this sucker – bringing forth, as Abraham Lincoln would famously declare, ' a new nation, conceived in Liberty and dedicated to the proposition that all men are created equal' – they all sat down and got pretty shitfaced. Celebrating the completion of the Declaration at, yes, a tavern, the 55 men got through more than 100 bottles of wine. Plus eight bottles of whiskey, eight bottles of hard cider and seven large bowls of spiked punch. And 22 bottles of porter. And 12 bottles of beer. The tavern's final bill included a surcharge for several broken tables, punch bowls and bottles … and, for some reason, a few broken chamber pots.

America, a land forged in liberty … by a bunch of guys who were all off their tits.

A RUM REBELLION
Why we are girt by rum

'Cut yer name across me backbone
Stretch me skin across yer drum
Iron me up on Pinchgut Island
From now to Kingdom Come.
I'll eat yer Norfolk Dumpling
Like a juicy Spanish plum,
Even dance the Newgate Hornpipe
If ye'll only gimme Rum.'

Convict drinking song

'Australians all let us rejoice, for we are young and free.' Setting aside the fact that we're home to the world's oldest living culture, there's not all that much wrong with the first sentence of the Australian national anthem. Where things go wrong is really right after that, when we're informed that 'Our home is girt by sea'.

'Girt,' let's face it, is just a silly word. But if you must use it, what's so great about sea? If you really want to celebrate some liquid's special role in our national story, then that liquid, my friends, should be rum.

Here's why. 1788. While the First Fleet contained around 1,500 convicts, settlers, soldiers and administrators, it only carried about £300 in cash. The expectation had been that the new colony would not actually need that much money once a few farms got up and running, because non-convicts could just trade, and be paid in, stuff like crops and supplies.

Unfortunately, it took farms over *two years* to get up and running, as nobody aboard seemed to be much of a farmer. The colonialists came very close to starvation, but – since the First Fleet had brought 800 gallons of rum for the ride – the good news was that no one got thirsty. Then an American ship arrived in Sydney with some much needed supplies ... and a further 7,597 gallons of rum.

'From the first settlement of New South Wales,' 19th century Australian writer Marcus Clarke tells us, 'the unrestrained importation of ardent spirits had prevailed to an alarming extent. Rum poured into the colony in barrels, in hogsheads, in puncheons. Rum flowed like water and was drunk like wine. Rum was taken morning, noon and night, was paid as 'boot' in exchanges, and received as payment for purchases ... Rum at last became a colonial currency. The governor, clergy, and officers civil and military, all bartered rum.'

Yes, that's right: 'a colonial currency'. With notes and coins in short supply, liquor was quite literally worth its weight in gold. If you wanted to barter for some goods or get a service performed, pay for some labour or be paid yourself, a glass, bottle or gallon of rum was generally in some way involved.

And so too were the NSW Police Corps. A patently corrupt regiment of soldiers sent over from England in the 1790s to help run the colony, these ne'er-do-wells became widely known as the 'Rum Corps' because … well, they were patently corrupt. In amongst various other rackets they would waylay every shipment of rum that sailed in, buy it all up at a bargain price and then 'exchange it for goods and labour at very favourable rates'.

It was a nudge-nudge, wink-wink sort of a system that soon had bureaucrats in London shaking their heads. So in 1807 they appointed a new governor to put an end to corruption, the 'violent, rash and tyrannical' Captain William Bligh.

A man who had already inspired one mutiny (on his now-famous old ship *The Bounty*), Bligh banned the rum trade in 1808 – and in so doing inspired a second. In an event now known as the Rum Rebellion, Australia's first and only military coup saw a furious Rum Corps march to Government House, find the valiant Governor Bligh hiding under his bed and promptly place him under arrest.

For the next year he could be found in prison, until Britain finally agreed to send another governor to take his place. Australians all let us rejoice, for we are girt by rum.

IN 19TH-CENTURY SYDNEY ...

'Drunkenness was a prevailing vice. Even children were to be seen in the streets intoxicated. On Sundays, men and women might be observed standing round the public-house doors, waiting for the expiration of the hours of public worship in order to continue their carousing. As for the condition of the prison population, that, indeed, is indescribable. Notwithstanding the severe punishment for sly grog selling, it was carried on to a large extent. Men and women were found intoxicated together, and a bottle of brandy was considered to be cheaply bought for 20 lashes ...'

'All that the vilest and most bestial of human creatures could invent and practise, was in this unhappy country invented and practised without restraint and without shame.'

For the Term of his Natural Life, Marcus Clarke, 1867

A TASTE OF SLAVERY
How alcohol has helped enslave millions

'When I read about the evils of drinking, I gave up reading.'

Henry Youngman

There's a lot of conflict in the world these days, but I think that there are at least two things that we can all agree on. The first is that snap-happy new mothers should be banned from Facebook, along with anyone who posts photos of food.

The second is that slavery is bad.

Which on the face of it, is also a black mark for rum. Not terribly popular outside of Queensland (though I imagine it also gets sales in Hell), rum essentially tastes like methylated spirits, but that's far from the worst of its crimes. Quite apart from the fact that it gives me bad headaches, and causes your more boganic types to get into brawls, this rough-as-guts drink has helped to enslave millions of men, women and children. (And did I mention that it gives me bad headaches?)

How? Here's how, in this sentence, right here: it was through a little something called the triangular trade. America's biggest business for a while there wasn't iPhones, soft drinks or unfunny sitcoms, or long Taylor Swift songs all about Taylor Swift. It was the undrinkable drink called rum. 'Rum was king of the colonies before the Revolutionary War,' according to the historian Ed Crews. By 1770, the (two million or so) colonials were distilling, buying and selling 4.8 million gallons of the stuff a year – and they were distilling it from a thing called molasses.

Essentially a sort of dense, black treacle, molasses is, of course, made from sugar cane, a plant that is labour-intensive to harvest and requires tropical conditions in order to grow. Tropical conditions such as those that you might find in the Caribbean. And intense labour such as that forced from slaves.

Long before all those cotton plantations you see in *Gone With the Wind*, slave ships were setting off from northern states to Africa filled with cloth, rifles and rum. They would trade these commodities for people in chains, then sail to the Caribbean Islands and sell these people to sugar plantations. Part of the payment for the slaves would involve sugar itself – or more likely its offshoot, molasses. And, as you might have guessed, they'd then take that molasses up north to the colonies, so it could be turned into rum ... and eventually traded for people in chains. Repeat that process 1000 times and you end up with one of the great crimes in history – a crime that's on par with the Holocaust and season four of *The Bachelor*.

Quite apart from the whole enslavement thing, it's worth noting that the triangular trade often meant murder: one in five Africans died on the journey across the Atlantic due to the simply appalling conditions on the ships. And I don't mean Jetstar appalling or youth hostel bad; I mean something *even worse*. For weeks and months at a time, men, women and children would be packed together below deck in 'foul', 'putrid' and dysentery-riddled conditions, in a space so tiny that most needed to crouch. 'The shrieks of the women and the groans of the dying, rendered the whole a scene of horror almost inconceivable,' former slave Olaudah Equiano later wrote in an essay that also touched on the 'loathsomeness of the stench', the 'heat of the climate', the 'pestilential filth' and the 'unmerciful floggings'. 'I ... wished for the last friend, death, to relieve me.'

It's enough to make rum leave a bad taste in your mouth – though for most people, it does that already.

DRINKING ~~TO~~ FOR YOUR HEALTH

How alcohol has saved thousands of lives

> 'People may say what they like about the decay of Christianity; the religious system that produced green Chartreuse can never really die.'
>
> Hector Hugh Munro

Whoever says that laughter is the best medicine clearly doesn't know much about cognac, a drink that can ward off the plague. Or indeed about absinthe: a great way to treat roundworms (as well as headaches, epilepsy and kidney stones). Gin, for its part, can cure pretty much any fever out there, and can be a great help if you have trouble in bowel country.

Any more? Well, sure. Vodka has been used to treat infertility, whiskey the common cold. Chartreuse was designed as a stomach tonic, Crème de Menthe as an aid for digestion. Benedictine, for its part, is a general elixir, much like wine mixed with laurel leaves and salt. Even Hippocrates, the Father of Medicine, prescribed vermouth for rheumatism. Alcohol has been a vital weapon in humanity's fight against disease.

Needless to say, the fight hasn't gone well. Alcohol has many wonderful qualities, but the ancient Babylonians were probably going a bit too far when they called it 'the head of medicines'. If the bubonic plague ever comes to Australia, and you find me half-dead and covered in pustules, I'd be very grateful if you could take me to a hospital, please, and not to the nearest pub.

But let's not be too dismissive of ancient wisdom, folks – because somewhere inside it, there was a small pinch of truth. While the 13th-century scholar Roger Bacon was wrong about pretty much everything, he was probably right to say that drinking a tankard of ale could 'defend the body from corruption' if it meant that you didn't drink anything else.

While hangovers and beer guts are both bad things, and nobody much likes liver damage, is any of that stuff really worse than the sort of things you can get from bad *water*? Are they worse than dysentery or typhoid, cholera or botulism? Or E. coli? Or Hepatitis A? For all its faults, alcohol is at least made with boiled water, and thus made with water that's clean. Whatever you might find in a bottle, what you definitely *won't* find is all those insidious little germy things that can make themselves at home in taps, ponds, pipes and wells. You won't find bacteria from rotting animals, or tiny organisms or stray bits of poo.

Don't just take my word for it, take Steven Johnson's. As that writer puts it, 'the search for unpolluted drinking water is as old as civilisation itself. As soon as there were mass human settlements, waterborne diseases like dysentery became a crucial population bottleneck. For much of human history, the solution to this chronic public-health issue was not purifying the water supply. The solution was to drink alcohol.'

It's worth pointing out that waterborne diseases were actually pretty rare in ancient times, thanks to the fact that most of Johnson's 'mass human settlements' were actually tiny villages where people could quench their thirst with clean rivers or wells. But they got a hell of a lot more common in the Middle Ages, as more and more country folk moved into the cities and were essentially forced to drink their own poo. Cholera epidemics, in particular, have killed tens of millions of people over the years, and continue to claim lives to this day.

Places like Paris and London would soon be at the forefront of industry and progress, but when it came to hygiene, they were badly behind. Medieval London, in particular, had no proper sewerage system. What it *did* have were 200,000 cesspits. And thousands of toilets that flushed straight into the Thames.

Well water looked bad and smelled bad because, by and large, it *was* bad – and the result was that people tried not to drink it. By the 16th century, the average British child drank 530 pints of beer a year, and the ones with responsible parents probably drank even more. Whether or not alcohol has 'saved millions of lives', as historians like Johnson insist, it's a safe bet that it's saved quite a few.

A HEALTHY ALTERNATIVE

'The introduction of beer into general use among the inhabitants would certainly lessen the consumption of spirituous liquors. I have therefore in conformity with your suggestion taken measures for furnishing the colony with a supply of ten tons of Porter, six bags of hops, and two complete sets of brewing materials.'

The Colonial Secretary, Lord Hobart, 1802

WHO DARES, WINS

How whiskey won a war

'Stay busy, get plenty of exercise, and don't drink too much. Then again, don't drink too little.'
— Herman Smith-Johannsen

The US Civil War wasn't civil at all. Roughly 2 per cent of Americans died during this four-year-long bloodbath, and many more suffered serious injuries. Brothers killed brothers, or uncles or sons, only to be killed in turn by some twice-removed second cousin. 'The Civil War left a culture of death, a culture of mourning, beyond anything Americans had ever experienced or imagined,' is how Dr David Blight puts it (though it's possible that Native Americans might imagine things differently).

What's interesting, however, is that the whole thing was a mismatch. It should have been over in a matter of months. There were, after all, over 22 million people in the North compared to just 9 million of their opponents in the South (of whom around half were slaves). The

North had more money, more factories, more soldiers and more ships. It produced something like 94 per cent of all the iron in the country, and close to 97 per cent of America's guns.

But what it *didn't* have, at first, were good generals. All the South needed to do, after it declared independence, was defend its borders for as long as it could on the off-chance that Abraham Lincoln et al would eventually give up. A war of attrition was in the slave owners' best interests, especially as the one thing they weren't short on was food.

It was, then, up to the North to attack. It was up to the North to throw caution to the wind and charge the South's superbly-organised blockades; to cross raging rivers while being cut down by cannon fire; to climb big mountains while being pelted with bombs.

But this was something that Lincoln's reportedly timid and uncertain generals comprehensively failed to do. They elected to fight only one major battle in the first year of the war, and it was a battle that they somehow managed to lose. It was the equivalent of an AFL team losing to an Under-12s side, or a team made up of people in comas.

But don't worry, all was well in the end. And it was thanks to a booze hound named Ulysses S Grant. Later elected president of the United States, and still the face of the country's $50 bill, Grant was, if truth be told, a little bit of a bum. When the war began Grant had already been kicked out of the army once for his excessive binge drinking, and had to re-enlist. 'That Grant drank occasionally while on duty is a matter of record, as is the fact that on more than a few occasions he drank until intoxicated, stuporous, and violently ill,' writes Edward G Longacre.

'He was, in the clinical sense of the term, an alcoholic. On more than a few occasions he drank long and hard, unable to stop short of unconsciousness or some form of intervention.'

But it turned out Grant's dash, flair and unpredictable I-don't-give-a-fuck-ness was exactly what the Northern army required. After being put in charge of a small infantry brigade, he racked up several big wins in a matter of months – together with several complaints about his incessant binge drinking.

'I can't spare this man. He fights,' was Abraham Lincoln's response to requests for his dismissal, requests that were instead met with several major promotions.

Grant's most famous (and, needless to say, casualty-rich) victory at the Battle of Vicksburg is generally regarded as the turning point of the war. He may have fallen off his horse, had his own private whiskey barrel and vomited in front of his troops at least twice, but on the other hand, he helped free the slaves.

And it may have been one hand that led to the other. 'In the end his predisposition to alcoholism may have made him a better general,' writes the historian James McPherson. 'His struggle for self-discipline enabled him to understand and discipline others; the humiliation of pre-war failures gave him a quiet humility that was conspicuously absent from so many generals with a reputation to protect; because Grant had nowhere to go but up, he could act with more boldness and decision than commanders who dared not risk failure.'

'I wish some of you would tell me the brand of whiskey that Grant drinks,' Lincoln once said after fielding yet another complaint about his secret weapon being a bit of a wino. 'I would like to send a barrel of it to my other generals.'

MEANWHILE, IN AUSTRALIA

No need for cultural cringing here, people: Australia has also had its fair share of alcohol-loving leaders. There is no greater example than Bob Hawke, of course, a man who got in the Guinness Book of World Records after swiftly sculling down a yard-long glass of beer. It all happened thanks to a much-loved tradition at Oxford called 'sconcing', which involved being publicly forced to drink from said glass as punishment for a breach of college etiquette. So when Bob turned up to the dining hall one day without his big, fancy gown, said punishment was duly imposed – and somehow completed in about ten seconds. According to Bob, 'This feat was to endear me to some of my fellow Australians more than anything else I ever achieved.'

THE ASSASSIN'S BEST FRIEND

How two presidents were lost due to drink

'Even though a number of people have tried, no one has yet found a way to drink for a living.'

Jean Kerr

The conscientious assassin should avoid drinking alcohol. If they are to take their job seriously, then history suggests they should instead smoke dope. We get the word 'assassin' from an Arabic proper noun meaning 'hashish-users'. 'Assassins' was the name given to a small group of professional killers in Persia, who apparently enjoyed a pipe or two in their downtime.

The conscientious bodyguard should also avoid drinking alcohol. The reason being, that it makes them crap at their job.

Abraham Lincoln is one person who'd need no persuading of this, and that's not just because he's now dead. The US president who freed the slaves was also a US president who loved watching plays. On 14 April 1865, just five days after the South formally surrendered in the US Civil War, that love took him to Ford's Theatre in Washington DC to see a well-reviewed farce called *Our American Cousin*.

His security detail was Constable John Parker, a policeman, according to writer Paul Martin, whose 'record as a cop fell somewhere between pathetic and comical'. Frequently charged with 'conduct unbecoming' (i.e. being drunk on the job), Parker was known to visit brothels while on duty and, every now and then, fall asleep on trams. So naturally enough, he'd been appointed President Lincoln's personal bodyguard – an unexpected promotion that clearly merited a drink.

So about halfway through the play, Parker went out and got one, leaving the war leader wholly unprotected and sitting with his back to a door. While at the Star Saloon, a little pub just next door, the bodyguard would have seen, and perhaps even talked to, a well-known Southern actor. A thespian who had once described whiskey as his very 'best friend', John Wilkes Booth was also busy getting pissed.

But unlike Constable Parker, Booth was not a man to neglect his duty. And being a proud Southerner, he naturally felt that that duty was to shoot the leader of the North. So – quite possibly after bidding Parker a cheerful 'goodnight' and promising to look him up on Facebook – that actor stumbled into Ford's Theatre and did just that before escaping into the night.

Of Constable Parker's next movements we have no further record, though it's said that in the morning he turned up at the police station 'arm-in-arm' with a local sex worker. 'Had he done his duty, I believe

President Lincoln would not have been murdered by Booth,' one of the bodyguard's colleagues later wrote in his memoirs. 'Parker knew that he had failed in duty. He looked like a convicted criminal the next day.'

'I did wrong, I admit, and have bitterly repented,' was the man himself's comment. 'I did not believe anyone would try to kill so good a man in such a public place, and the belief made me careless.'

Mysteriously, he managed to keep his position for three more months, before once again falling asleep on the job and being fired for his troubles.

You couldn't accuse JFK's bodyguards of being overly sleepy, however. Their problem was that they hardly slept at all. On the night before Kennedy was killed in Dallas, nine of the 28 agents assigned to protect him were boozing at pub called The Cellar until the wee hours. Six of them stayed until three in the morning, and a seventh stuck around until five. All started work before eight.

'The biggest problem I ran into with the Secret Service when I was an agent was their constant drinking,' an agent from that time later told *Vanity Fair*. 'When we would get to a place one of the first things they would do was stock up with liquor. They would drink and then we would go to work. Their reflexes were affected by ... the loss of sleep ... and amount of alcohol.' He also described hearing a fellow agent shout out, 'I told those playboys that someone was going to get the president killed if they kept acting like they did.'

That guy sounds like a bit of a downer – but, as it happens, he was also correct. The first shot fired by Lee Harvey Oswald that fateful day in

Dallas happened to miss Kennedy completely. And the second shot also failed to kill him. No less than four full seconds then elapsed before that fatal third shot was fired, four seconds in which JFK's driver should have swerved the car, or sped it up. Four seconds during which the agents running on either side of his car, and sitting in its front seat, should have leaped on and covered his body.

But instead, in the words of another agent, all but two of the bodyguards 'just basically sat there with their thumbs up their butts while the president was gunned down in front of them'. According to another observer, they practically 'seemed paralysed'.

Why? Well, 'don't you think that if a man went to bed reasonably early, and hadn't been drinking the night before he would be more alert than if he stayed up until three or five o'clock in the morning going to beatnik joints and doing some drinking along the way?' That question was asked by Chief Justice Earl Warren during his famous inquiry into the assassination several months later. He noted that a few bystanders had even been able to see Oswald's gun pointing out of a sixth-floor window, less than 80 metres from the motorcade, for quite a few seconds before it was fired.

'Some people saw a rifle up in that building. Wouldn't a Secret Service man in this motorcade, who is supposed to observe such things, be more likely to observe something of that kind if he was free from any of the results of liquor or lack of sleep than he would otherwise? Don't you think that they would have been more alert, sharper?'

Maybe. And JFK might now be more alert too …

GREAT AUSTRALIAN PISS-UPS

Julian O'Neill, 1999

'I shat in Schlossy's shoe.'

The former NRL player fesses up during a big night in Dubbo.

Mark Gasnier, 2004

'Where the fuck are you? There's four toey humans in the cab. It's twenty to four ... and you're in bed, fuck me. Fire up, you sad cunt.'

A message left on a woman's answering machine by NRL star Mark Gasnier during a night on the turps.

Nate Myles, 2009

'It was dark and I was a bit dazed. The door to the toilet was right next to the entry door and I went through the wrong one.'

The Sydney Rooster after a night allegedly spent partying until 4am – and pooing in a hotel corridor.

Joel Monaghan, 2009

'It was a moment of abject stupidity brought about by too much drink and a complete lack of any thought process.

'Joel can't blame anyone but himself for an act of stupidity that will haunt him for the rest of his life. Joel wants to make it clear that he was the one playing a prank on an absent teammate by simulating the act.'

The NRL's player's manager after his charge decided to feign sex with a dog.

Mitchell Pierce, 2009

'I'll fuck that dog, I don't give a fuck. I don't have a sexuality.'

Another NRL star with an unusual idea of fun.

Todd Carney, 2014

'Todd's paid a very, very heavy price for a photo that he didn't want out there or upload himself. It was supposed to be kept between mates.'

Todd Carney's agent after the NRL player was snapped 'bubbling' at a Sydney nightclub.

MILK-BORNE ILLNESS BE GONE

How sour wine saved the world

'Wine is the most healthful and most hygienic of beverages.'

— Louis Pasteur

Accidentally overhearing Justin Bieber isn't the only thing in life that can leave a sour taste in your mouth. Bad wine can have the exact same effect. Leave a bottle open too long and all sorts of little bacteria bustle in, turning this sweet, delicious nectar of the gods into something not unlike Satan's anus.

But that's just common sense, yes?

No sir, not at all. Until the mid-19th century – roughly 6000 years after the world's oldest-known wine press was built – humanity had no idea what made this good thing go bad. It took a great man to tackle the issue, and that great man was Napoleon III. Best remembered for rebuilding Paris, modernising the banks and I would imagine all sorts of other stuff, that ruler's *real* achievement was hiring an obscure French chemist to investigate a vital social question: why did so many fine wines keep going sour?

As one merchant noted at the time, that country's wine industry had just been having a bad decade 'because of the disease to which they are subject,' which caused 'great losses and endless troubles'. Pasteur noted that 'there may not [have been] a single winery in France, whether rich or poor, where some portions of the wine [had] not suffered greater or lesser alteration'.

Anyway, back to this obscure rural chemist – whose name happened to be Louis Pasteur. Pasteur began a two-year investigation into the microscopic mysteries of fermentation that produced a little practice we call pasteurisation. In essence, he discovered that if you boil up a liquid, immediately cool it down, then seal it up and store somewhere airless and cool, you'll kill all these invisible little things that might be lurking inside it – invisible little things that we now call 'bacteria'.

The French wine industry was accordingly saved.

But the big story is that so were millions of lives. Pasteur's study of wine and beer went far, far beyond wine and beer; it basically made him the father of all modern medicine. Because bacteria, of course, doesn't just cause *drinks* to go bad, it does the same thing to the human body. Pasteur may not have been the first person to propose the existence of 'germs', but he was the man who essentially proved their existence. 'His germ theory became the foundation upon which hygienic principles of medical care were based.'

And let's not forget, we also pasteurise *milk*. Milk-borne illnesses including tuberculosis, salmonella, typhoid fever and diphtheria used to kill millions of people every year. These days, however, we don't get sick from milk. (Unless we're stupid enough to leave it out of the fridge or – worse – buy an Eggnog Big M.)

So let's all raise a glass to Louis Pasteur. Then find some soap and go scrub our hands.

CARNIVOROUS COCKTAILS

Bacteria isn't the only 'living' thing you might find in your drink. Here are some beverages with unusually meaty ingredients that probably won't tickle your fancy.

- Cambodian tarantula brandy
- Korean baby mice rice wine
- Chinese three penis wine
- Thai snake whiskey
- Icelandic topas (vodka) with rotting shark

THE BIRTH OF A NATION

How Australia's first battle might been over beer

'When you get tight in foreign lands,
All foreigners are brothers—
You drink their drink and grasp their hands
And never wish for others.
Their foreign ways and foreign songs—
And girls—you take delight in:
The war-whoop that you raise belongs
To the country you get tight in.'

'The Foreign Drunk', Henry Lawson

Gallipoli was more than a military campaign. It was Australia's baptism of fire. Taking place, as it did, just 14 short years after Federation, it represented the very first time we ever sent troops to fight for *us*, as a nation. The first time Aussies had marched underneath our own flag, wearing slouch hats, Southern-Cross badges, and so on. When those first shots were fired on the beaches of Turkey, we in some deep sense ceased to be just an outpost of England, and became a real country, in our own right.

Or so, at least, say historians. 'There was a tragic notion at the time that even though we had a constitution, even though we were federated, even though we had a parliament and all the rest, we weren't a real nation until we had shed blood,' says Peter FitzSimons. While for Robert Manne, 'the [Anzac] story gave the sense that Australia was born as a nation, because it had shown itself in the eyes of Britain not to be compromised by the convict stain, but as courageous, manly, and effective militarily.'

And Manne certainly isn't the only man who says, feels and thinks stuff like this. For some white-faced, orange-haired, red-necked types, Anzac Day has become a sort of de facto Australia Day. The day our boys arrived on those Turkish-soldier-strewn beaches is now the time to grab hold of a flag and then use it to stab a few immigrants. If you ever wanted to organise a race riot, 25 April would be the ideal time.

But perhaps we should move the day forward a few weeks? Perhaps Anzac Day should be on 2 April? For Australia's first true taste of battle – the first time that we actually spilt blood on foreign soil – was not on the beaches of Turkey at all, but in Cairo, on the banks of the Nile. The Australian character was shown to the world for what it was at a little something called the Battle of the Wazzir.

Though 'battle,' perhaps, is a generous term. Strictly speaking, it was more like a riot. 'The night before we left ... there was a big row in the (brothel district of) Wazza,' is how one unrepentant digger remembered it. 'Our chaps and the New Zealanders pulled and burned half of it down, pianos, chairs, tables, women and all went out the window. As soon as they hit the ground, on the fire they went. It would have been a good thing if they had burned every bit of it to the ground.'

Roughly 2500 Anzacs took part in the riot that followed – a riot that resulted in the death of at least three Egyptians. They set brothels alight, tore down houses and shops, and seriously injured a few dozen residents.

The local police tried to intervene but they were soon driven back with 'heavy missiles such as tables and big logs of wood'. The British army itself was eventually forced to step in, sending out a few mounted squadrons to help quell the disturbance.

What the hell caused the riot is still debated to this day, though it's safe to say that relations with the locals up until that point hadn't necessarily been that warm. ('We thrash the black fellows with whips,' was how one Anzac described their approach to diplomacy. 'Every nigger who is impudent to a soldier gets a hiding ... I can't say how many I've belted and knocked out.') Some say that the Anzacs were angry because many of the brother soldiers had gone and got STIs from the brothels; others because a brothel had been watering down the booze, and/or secretly adding some urine.

The short answer is that we simply don't know – but what we *do* know is that they were all pretty drunk. 'Like any large event that takes place that involves a lot of people and a lot of fractious behaviour, the memories (of what exactly caused the riot) are both selective and self-serving,' says the commentator Michael Caulfield. Ultimately, all we can say for certain is it happened for 'the same reason you get trouble on George Street on a Saturday night: a lot of young guys, a lot of testosterone, a lot of booze'.

Young men and alcohol can make for a violent combination. Or, in this case, for the birth of a nation.

NEVER DRINK ALONE

'All through Australia, in every class, it is not considered good form for a man to drink by himself. Very few even of the most hopeless drunkards ever do so. The consequence is, that when a man feels inclined to drink, he immediately looks out for someone to drink with. At whatever hour of the day a man meets another whom he has not seen for say twelve hours, etiquette requires that he shall incontinently invite him to come and drink. This is a custom that pervades every class in the colony, and cannot be departed from without something more than a breach of good manners.'

Finch Hatton 1887

~~DUTCH~~ TURKISH COURAGE

Did liquor lose us Gallipoli?

'Alcohol is a misunderstood vitamin.'

PG Wodehouse

Playing the pokies. Chucking a sickie. Suddenly caring about swimming during the Summer Olympics. Australia is a land full of heart-warming traditions – little customs that you could call green and gold.

In recent times, going to Anzac Cove on 25 April has become one of them – so long as you go there to get shitfaced. The Australian Defence Force has expressed concerns about 'the increasingly excessive use of alcohol during Anzac Day commemorations' at the site – and they're concerns that the Turkish Government clearly shares. It's now illegal to raise a glass at the place where 8700 Aussies went down.

Mind you, a lot of Turks went down too. 'I don't order you to fight, I order you to die,' was how their frontline general presented his KPIs the day that our boys came ashore. And thousands of Turkish soldiers performed just as he expected, in an effort to keep our Anzacs contained. 'In the time it takes us to die, other troops and commanders can come and take our places,' was his somewhat deflating take on affairs that first day, as the Australians began to push their way inland. Personally, I'd prefer a general who said, 'Fuck this, let's run' – or who'd at least let me call in a sickie.

Anyway, where were we? Oh yes: that crazy-brave general who stopped the invaders in their tracks on what we all now like to call Anzac Day. His equally suicidal regiment forced a retreat, retook the high ground and hung onto it until reinforcements arrived.

And there they stayed for eight long months, easily repelling every Anzac attack from below. Eventually, of course, the Anzacs were forced to give up, and sail off to Europe to try and win the war there. That single moment of Turkish heroism had doomed the entire Allied campaign.

So who was this Turkish hero? He was Mustafa Kemal, a man best known as 'Ataturk'. Eventually elected his country's first president, he went on to abolish the sultanate and establish a secular Turkish democracy. You can still see his words on plaques all over Australia. 'Wipe away your tears,' the Father of the Turks told Australia's mothers. 'Your sons are now lying in our bosom and are in peace. After having lost their lives on this land they have become our sons as well … (The) heroes that shed their blood and lost their lives … are now lying in the soil of a friendly country.' Uplifting stuff, I'm sure you'll agree, even though there are some doubts as to whether he actually said it.

But one thing that we *can* be sure he said is, 'Another drink, please. Actually, two drinks. No, let's make it four. Or, rather, eight.' Raki (a sort of aniseed-flavoured milky-white spirit) is like vodka, only quite a bit stronger – and it's a drink that Ataturk got through a litre of every day of his life. Also fond of coffee and cigarettes (we're talking fifteen cups and three packs a day), he died of cirrhosis of the liver at age 57, and the only wonder was that he didn't die earlier.

A *New York Times* journalist once remarked that Turkey was 'run by a drunk and 20 bandits'. Ataturk promptly fired off a letter in reply. The allegation was not true, he wrote, Turkey was run by a drunk.

We don't know how much was in his system on 25 April, that fateful day when he stood on the front line, stared death in the face and said 'charge', but you'd have to suspect it was a shitload. If the Turkish Government's anti-alcohol laws had been in place way back then, would there now be a Turkey at all?

WORDS FOR DRUNK

Drunk people can behave in all sorts of ways (though I myself am invariably charming). This may help explain why we have all sorts of words to describe them. Here I give you some of the best:

'arseholed', 'bibulous', 'bory eyed', 'Brahms and Liszt', 'bumpsy', 'drunk as a lord', 'ebrious', 'full as a goog', 'goosed', 'got yer wobbly boots on', 'half cut', 'howling', 'in your cups', 'jober as a sudge', 'lit like a Christmas tree', 'lush', 'moory', 'munted', 'one over the eight', 'out of your box', 'Podgy', 'pie-eyed', 'rat-legged', 'pissed as a newt', 'schnooked', 'squiffed', 'somewhat the worse for wear', 'three sheets to the wind', 'top heavy', 'tired and emotional', 'woofled'.

THE NOBLE EXPERIMENT

How Prohibition helped make the mob

'Once, during Prohibition, I was forced to live for five days on nothing but food and water.'

WC Fields

Have you ever wondered how organised crime got so *very* organised? How a few fat blokes who had to move their mouths when they read suddenly found themselves in charge of great, big global empires, with lawyers and accountants and warehouses and planes and secret bank accounts and God knows what else? Running a mob these days is a major commitment – you need more than just a cool nickname.

If we had to put a date on this development, it would be 1920. Criminals before then hadn't really got it together. Even the Mafia, once you got outside Sicily, wasn't so much a sinister global enterprise as a loose network of fairly small-time gangs. America had always had thuggish types with guns who hang out in groups and get involved in prostitution, 'protection' and theft, but none of them had ever operated on a particularly grand scale. If they'd been able to afford a financial adviser, he'd probably have suggested they get a real job.

So what happened in 1920? I'll give you just one word (albeit a long one) and that word is 'Prohibition'. Known as the 'Volsted Act', after the ever-so-religious Republican who steered it through Congress, this inspired piece of legislation made booze illegal in the US – and it made everyone who was still willing to sell it extraordinarily rich.

Alcohol, until that point, had been the nation's fifth-biggest industry: the US had thousands of breweries, wineries and distilleries selling their wares to an even greater number of pubs, clubs and restaurants. And for the 13 years that Prohibition stayed in place, alcohol continued to be the nation's fifth-biggest industry – but during that time, it was all underground. Gangs simply took over the making, storing and selling of alcohol. And when the alcohol-free clubs and pubs folded for lack of business, they simply launched 'speakeasies' too.

'Bosses' like Al Capone reportedly raked in about $100 million a year, entirely free of tax – profits that would be counted in billions today if we factored in things like inflation. 'I'm just a businessman giving the public what they want,' he used to say, not unreasonably.

And like all big-businessmen, he needed plenty of staff.

'It took significant organisation to bootleg the quantities of alcohol people desired,' writes Daniel Florien. 'The result was organised crime, which didn't differentiate between petty crimes like transporting liquor and real crimes like violence, murder, and theft.' Bribes had to be paid and money had to be laundered. Smugglers needed to smuggle and enforcers had to enforce. What this meant was that rag-tag street gangs slowly became large-scale, sophisticated enterprises, with control over unions, connections to government, and casinos, brothels and speakeasies in every town.

And after that, came accountants as well. As noted by Bill Norris, 'The profits – and associated violence to steal and protect those profits – led the Mafia to actually sit down and create a structure to keep the money flowing and the internal bloodshed to a minimum. Suddenly there were rules in place to keep the criminal enterprises running smoothly and methods to resolve disputes other than the business end of a Tommy Gun.'

So what did these suddenly organised criminals do when 'the Noble Experiment' ended? When buying and selling alcohol ceased to be a crime? They simply took their 20 per cent share of the American economy and invested the profits elsewhere. In drugs and gambling. In pimping and protection. In loan sharking and murder-for-hire.

And their descendants are still doing these things today. El Chapo wouldn't have been much chop had it not been for Al Capone.

TRICKY LIQUOR LAWS

Prohibition is long gone in the US, and only barely got a foot in the door Down Under. But there are several countries where drinking is still just not done, including Afghanistan, Iran, Libya, Saudi Arabia, Sudan and Yemen. But there are other, far stranger liquor laws out there:

- You can't ride a cow if you're drunk (Scotland)
- It's illegal to buy alcohol in the morning (Thailand)
- It's illegal to drink on election day (Turkey)
- Minors can drink (Alaska)
- Only the government may sell booze with an alcohol percentage over 3.5 (Sweden)

MAKING A MURDERER

Did alcohol help fuel the Holocaust?

'The first glass is a sedative, the second a psychologist, the third glass an excuse, and the fourth a lobotomy.'

Terri Guillemets

If you're looking for a light and breezy read, the diary of an SS soldier isn't such a great choice. 'Shooting of big batches has started once again,' proceeds an entry from one. 'Today about four thousand people were driven up, shot by 80 executioners, all drunk. This time terrible tortures before shooting. Nobody buried the murdered. The people were driven straight into the pit, the corpses were trampled upon. Many a wounded writhed with pain. Nobody finished them off.'

Another entry from another diary: 'The condemned were stripped of their clothes. In groups of 300 they were forced into the ditches. First, they threw in the children. The women were shot at the edge of the ditch, after that it was the turn of the men ... All the men doing the shooting were drunk.'

One of the great and enduring mysteries of the Holocaust is simply this: how the hell did it happen? How did so many seemingly ordinary men and women suddenly turn into cold-blooded killers? Six million murders requires hundreds of thousands of murderers, but surely they can't *all* have been born psychopathic. For every certifiable maniac, like Hitler or Himmler, there must have been dozens of mild-mannered accountants and chefs who somehow woke up one day sans a conscience.

But *how*?

One of the answers could well be alcohol. While 'abstinence' was one of the nine 'virtues of the SS man', according to the far-away-from-the-killing-fields Führer, 'unlimited quantities of liquor' were actually made 'freely available' to pretty much every concentration camp guard. 'It was all fun and entertainment, just like a small town,' said one such guard about Auschwitz, of all places. 'Alcohol played a big role ... (and we often) went to bed completely pissed ... When somebody was too lazy to turn off the light, we just shot it out. And nobody said anything about the bullet holes in the walls.'

Or, indeed, the bullet holes in the prisoners. One survivor of Treblinka recalled plenty of 'SS-men who held a pistol or truncheon in one hand, (and a) whiskey bottle in the other.'

Vodka and schnapps also played 'a big role' in the Einsatzgruppen, the paramilitary death squads that were sent out into enemy territory to shoot Jews, Gypsies, Slavs, priests, intellectuals, and pretty much anyone with any sort of disability. 'In many testimonies on mass murders of Jews by SS and German police units in the East, witnesses and perpetrators mention that alcohol was present or that the killers were intoxicated,' writes Edward B Westermann.

'We have to carry out this unhappy task, shooting all the way to the Urals,' is how one SS officer answered a new recruit when he was asked why everyone was so drunk. 'As you can imagine, it's not pretty and one can bear it only with alcohol.'

An account of a mass killing in Poland describes many of the perpetrators as having been 'depressed, angered, embittered, and shaken' after the event. 'They ate little but drank heavily. Generous quantities of alcohol were provided, and many ... got quite drunk.'

All in all, as Westermann puts it, it would seem that the 'abuse of alcohol ... served multiple functions' in the Holocaust's history-making abuse of human rights, 'from steadying the nerves to lowering inhibitions or exaggerating existing prejudices. As such it facilitated physical abuse, sexual transgression, and mass murder.'

Notorious SS figures who we know to have been alcoholics include Paul Blobel ('a drunk and a monster' responsible for 59,018 murders) and Oskar Dirlewanger, a paedophile, supposed necrophile and notorious sadist whose 'leadership was characterised by constant alcohol abuse'. Once described as 'the vilest individual in the vilest organisation ever known', Odilo Globočnik was also one of the drunkest, and Ernst Kaltenbrunner, the leader of the Austrian SS, was a man who 'couldn't go a half-hour without a drink'.

All four of these monsters would still have been monsters when sober. But can we confidently say that about the entire SS?

> **NOT ALL MURDERERS**
>
> There've been plenty of alcoholic killers through history: Ted Bundy, Jeffery Dahmer, John Wayne Gracey, Gilbert Paul Jordon and Henry Lee Lucas, just to name a few. But one of Australia's most famous killers took quite a different approach. In 2002, Chopper Read, the infamous Melbourne underground figure who once admitted to 'between four and seven murders' popped up in a drink-driving ad. Showing off the scars of various injuries received in prison, he declared that 'If you drink and drive and you're unfortunate enough to hit somebody, you ought to pray to God that you don't go to prison.'

THE BIG THREE (DRINKERS)

How alcohol helped defeat the Führer

'Remember gentlemen, it's not just France we're fighting for, it's Champagne!'

Winston Churchill

Forget the Fantastic Four and the Famous Five, the Secret Six and the Magnificent Seven. When it comes to *actually* saving the world, the Big Three have got them all beat. Also known as 'Winston Churchill', 'Josef Stalin' and 'Franklin D Roosevelt', the three leaders of the Allied war effort, the Big Three's willingness to overcome their differences and fight Hitler together was what ultimately won World War II.

'So how did they overcome their differences?' you ask, Well, even if you didn't, I'd like to give you the answer.

It's alcohol. While Hitler was a confirmed teetotaller (a lifestyle choice shared by Donald Trump that may in some small way help explain both men's rage), his three main rivals all enjoyed their alcoholic refreshments – and, indeed, seem to have been refreshed rather a lot of the time.

Churchill, for his part, was a full-blown alcoholic. England's prime minister may well have been capable of going a day without 15 or 20 drinks, but we'll never know because he never gave it a go. 'There is always some alcohol in his blood,' observed one acquaintance, 'and it reaches its peak late in the evening after he has had two or three scotches, several glasses of champagne, at least two brandies and a highball.' Fond of starting every day with what he called his 'mouthwash' – that being a stiffish whiskey and soda – Winston cheerfully admitted to drinking 'champagne at all meals, and buckets of claret and soda in between'.

President Roosevelt, meanwhile, was the man who repealed Prohibition – and then immediately celebrated by draining a beer. The president was 'oftentimes carried off to his White House bedroom by Secret Service men while he chanted college fight songs,' writes journalist Brian Abrams. According to US historians he liked to have a drink with White House guests every single night of his presidency.

Which brings us to Stalin, a man who was supposedly wrapped in vodka-soaked rags as a child in order to dull teething pains. Whether or not that particular story's true, the Soviet leader certainly liked a strong drink or six, and was famous for hosting 'debauched dinners' every single night of his reign. That 'tyrannical toastmaster' would make his guests stand up and slam down around 30 vodka shots each, just to see them sweat, wobble and sway. It's said that when Hitler broke their non-aggression pact and launched an invasion of Russia, Stalin retreated to his dacha and stayed drunk for a week. He was certainly missing in action when needed most at the Kremlin.

But back to the Big Three, and the strange bond between them. Also missing in action, as far as Britain was concerned, was America in the first few years of the war. While that country certainly ~~profiteered~~ helped where it could when it came to food and supplies, actual US soldiers were conspicuously absent. That changed after the Japanese bombed Pearl Harbor, but the fact that Roosevelt promptly declared war on Germany as well as Japan came down in large part to his friendship with Churchill.

And just like most of my friendships, it was one very much formed in booze. Churchill met with Roosevelt a number of times during the early years of the war to try and persuade him to take some part in it. Technically known as 'benders', the bulk of these meetings took place during what White House staff came to call 'Winston hours' – the brandy-soaked early hours of the morning. 'It was noted that, afterward, FDR slept for 10 hours a night, three days in a row, to recuperate.'

Churchill's bond with Stalin also came down to booze – and this was a bond that was not easy to form. While the UK and the US were in many ways natural allies, communist Russia was anything but. A stalwart Tory, Churchill had been speaking out against the Soviet Union since the day it was formed, and as far as Stalin was concerned, his failure to share information and open up a proper 'second front' against the Germans meant that he was undermining it still. The fragile alliance was tested in August 1942 when the two sides met to thrash out their differences. And it may well have fractured had Churchill not suggested that he and Stalin abandon their staff members and retire to Stalin's room for one or two private drinks.

At around three in the morning, one of Churchill's secretaries entered the room and found 'Winston and Stalin and [the Soviet Foreign Minister] Molotov ... sitting with a heavily-laden board between them: food of all kinds crowned by a sucking pig and innumerable bottles. What Stalin made me drink seemed pretty savage: Winston, who by that time was complaining of a slight headache, seemed wisely to be confining himself to a comparatively innocuous, effervescent, Caucasian red wine. Everyone seemed to be as merry as a marriage bell.'

'I think the two great men really made contact and got on terms,' the secretary later reflected. 'Certainly, Winston was impressed and I think that feeling was reciprocated ... Anyhow, conditions have been established in which messages exchanged between the two will mean twice as much, or more, than they did before.'

So hooray for alcohol, I think we should say – and its best work was still to come. I am, of course, talking about the most famous meeting between the Big Three: the destiny-of-mankind-deciding Conference at Yalta. Called to decide how Europe might be carved up after the war, and to ensure Soviet support in the fight with Japan, the 1945 meeting was held in the middle of an ice-cold winter at a tiny Russian resort town with next to no toilets. Surrounded by 'bombed out buildings, rotting animal carcasses, destroyed tanks and torn-up railroad tracks', Yalta's tiny, rundown hotels didn't offer much in the way of mod-cons, but they weren't short on mozzies, bedbugs and lice. Staffers were packed six to nine in a room, on paper-thin mattresses that were 'so thin (one) could feel the springs'. 'We could have not have found a worse place if we spent ten years on research,' a dejected Churchill remarked on arrival.

But don't worry, everyone soon cheered up, and that's because there was no shortage of booze. Churchill himself brought along 500 cigars and drank enough 'buckets of Caucasian champagne to undermine the health of any normal man'. Like the Americans, he also appreciated the 'gallons and gallons' of fine Ukrainian wine that Stalin ordered in for the occasion, along with glasses of brandy that were served throughout every meeting and the decanters of vodka sent to rooms every night. The Soviet leader also gave a number of 'very friendly and gay' parties, with innumerable toasts – innumerable toasts that 'resulted in many inebriated Brits and Americans having to be carried back to their rooms'.

Rooms that we now know were bugged. Did the Soviet agents listening in hear any diplomatic secrets get drunkenly spilled, secrets that may have helped Stalin in his negotiations? We will probably never know. But what we do know is that Stalin's negotiations certainly went well. When World War II finished, he found himself in charge of Eastern Europe – prompting what historians now call the Cold War.

MEANWHILE IN AUSTRALIA

'So where was our prime minister in all this', you might be asking. 'Why wasn't it the Big Three and a Quarter?' Well, apart from the undeniable fact that we weren't powerful, populous, wealthy or influential enough to demand our leader be wooed with booze, boozing was something our prime minister preferred to avoid, in a flagrant betrayal of stereotype. John Curtin had struggled with alcoholism and depression as a young man, and his early career had suffered as a result. In the words of one of his colleagues, 'John Curtin sober was the finest bloke alive. John Curtin drunk was a vicious cur.'

Like another Labor PM, Bob Hawke, some forty years later, he had to pledge to get clean in order to get on in politics, and secure the support from his colleagues that would place him on top. By the time he was prime minister, Curtin was stone-cold sober, and a Big Three booze-fest wouldn't have been his scene.

REDS IN THE BED AND DRINKS IN THE SINK

How McCarthyism began with a bottle

'If drinking is interfering with your work, you're probably a heavy drinker. If work is interfering with your drinking, you're probably an alcoholic.'

Anonymous

These days, 'Black Magic' is a slightly overpriced chocolate box – a 'classic collection' by Nestlé that's filled with 'flowing golden caramels' and 'dark chocolate shells', together with 'whole roasted hazelnuts set in a heavenly praline'. I can't say that its occult properties are immediately evident but, if history is any guide to these things, I also can't say that this matters.

'Black Magic', you see, used to be a bit like 'beauty': it existed only in the eye of the beholder. If any medieval peasants wanted to find out whether some local chick was a witch, they wouldn't look for evidence of actual, you know, *spells* and so forth, they would just tie her up and toss her into a river. If she didn't drown, then there was clearly some sort of sorcery at work, with the result that she was burned at the stake. But the good news for the accused was that if she *did* indeed drown, then she was declared innocent, without a stain on her character. As an approach to justice, it was not without flaws, but on the upside, it was highly efficient.

Joe McCarthy was also efficient. The US senator used not dissimilar techniques throughout the 1950s, while accusing more or less every single person on the planet of being some sort of communist spy. If a person denied it, then they were obviously guilty, for what kind of a spy would admit it? And if McCarthy couldn't find any proof, then that was proof in itself, for what kind of spy would leave evidence lying around? Described by journalist Nicholas Von Hoffman as 'a loutish, duplicitous bully who carried, not the names of Reds but bottles of hooch in his briefcase' (and Hoffman was relatively sympathetic to Joe's cause), that Cold War warrior fed on paranoia and fear to ruin lives and careers – and washed it all down with gallons of scotch.

He first came to fame in 1950, after an undistinguished couple of years in the Senate. The catalyst was Joe's announcement that the State Department contained over 200 'secret communists'. At a small party for Republicans, a soused McCarthy made a short speech holding up a probably blank piece of paper. 'While I cannot take the time to name all the men in the State Department who have been named as members of the Communist Party and members of a spy ring,' he announced, 'I have here in my hand a list of 205. A list of names that were known to the secretary of state and who, nevertheless, are still working and shaping policy of the State Department.'

A few boozy hours later, he gave the same speech elsewhere – only this time (liquor leading to memory loss and all), the number had somehow become 58. Either way, though, that was more than enough spies – and certainly enough to guarantee McCarthy five years of media coverage and the chairmanship of a sort of spy-catching committee, with full presidential support.

But that support faded a touch after he failed to catch any actual spies – and then started flinging accusations at the president himself. A classic victim of crazed over-reach, the senator was eventually stripped of his chairmanship, censured by the Senate and condemned by the media, before dying of hepatitis at age 48.

What on earth was he thinking? A better question may be: what was he *drinking*? For the historian James Graham, 'McCarthy was an alcoholic, and his alcoholism explains his infamous behaviour.'

'He had always been a heavy drinker,' agrees journalist Richard Rovere, 'and there were times in those [later years] when he drank more than ever ... He was not always drunk, he went on the wagon (for him this meant beer instead of whiskey) for days and weeks at a time. [But] the difficulty towards the end was that he couldn't hold the stuff. He went to pieces on his second or third drink.'

And then he started in on his fourth, fifth and sixth.

GREAT AUSTRALIAN PISS-UPS

Ian Chappell, 1978

'I was leaning back in my chair at the time and, when he pushed me in the chest, I fell backwards. As I got up, he suggested we settle it outside. I replied: "I don't fight. You either finish up in jail or hospital and I don't intend visiting either over an arsehole like you." I turned and headed outside where he yelled something about knocking my block off on the cricket field the next day.'

Cricket legend Ian Chappell on a run-in with Ian Botham at a Melbourne pub.

David Boon, 1989

'I know there are plenty of stories flying around about me that have been greatly embellished over the years.

'But that's how it is ... we played our cricket in an era where blokes learned never to let the truth get in the way of a good story.'

Former cricketer David Boon on the infamous flight to England that supposedly saw him drink 52 beers.

Ricky Ponting, 1999

'I had had a few drinks and I had a few more drinks, until it was getting late. I'd apparently bumped into a guy at the bar and spilt his drink on him and ended up with a black eye the next morning.

'Telling the team manager half the story because I wasn't sure about the rest of the night and where it had gone was a pretty hard thing to do, because it came across as if I was holding something back and not telling the whole truth.

'But to be totally honest I didn't really have a great recollection of what had taken place.'

Former Test captain Ricky Ponting after a largish night in Kings Cross that saw him dance with a drag queen and get beaten up by another patron.

BOMB THE SHIT OUT OF THEM!

How Nixon's drinking nearly started a war

'Always do sober what you said you'd do drunk. That will teach you to keep your mouth shut.'

Ernest Hemingway

The United States has a Lincoln Memorial and a Washington Monument, a JFK Airport and a Jefferson City. There's an Eisenhower High School and a Barack Obama Boulevard, a Bill Clinton School of Public Service and a Ronald Reagan Highway.

Memorials to Richard M Nixon, however, remain curiously thin on the ground. Forced to leave the White House in 1974 thanks to a little something called 'Watergate', Tricky Dicky has been described as 'vindictive', 'paranoid', 'sly' and 'corrupt' – and that's just to quote his best friends. If you want a mental image, imagine Donald Trump with an extra 50 IQ points, 75 times more subtlety and regular-sized hands.

Before he won the presidency in 1968, some also described Nixon as a raving, vicious drunk. But don't worry, that was all set to change. As the Republican candidate told a journalist at the time, he was very much planning to live 'like a Spartan' once the nuclear codes were placed in his hands. 'You can't drink and think clearly,' Dicky reassured Theodore White, ironically while clutching a whiskey. 'Two drinks and your mind isn't quite sharp, and you may not be able to think clearly when that phone rings at night ... You've got to be ready.' Getting into the White House would mean 'no more drinking and no more late hours ... [I feel I know] what Jefferson meant when he said the presidency was a "splendid misery"'.

Well, let's just call it a misery. Newly-elected-president Nixon's commitment to sobriety ultimately lasted for less than one day – though in fairness, he did wait until evening. Also fond of drinking during the afternoon, or when alone, or when around other people, journalist Brian Abrams reported that the leader of the free world became notorious for 'drunk dialling people in his cabinet, his staff, or his old football coach' every night 'until he'd mumble himself to sleep'.

Though getting to sleep could sometimes take quite a while. 'He was given to exploding ... if he had had a few drinks,' Nixon's deputy assistant secretary of state once recalled. 'He would call up [secretary of state] Bill Rogers or somebody else and say, "Fire this man" ... Bill said Nixon would forget this the next morning.'

Other times, however, the message would be 'fire this *bomb*'. 'If the president had his way, there would be a nuclear war each week!' Rogers's successor, Henry Kissinger, is said to have sometimes growled to his aides. 'I could leave this room and in 25 minutes, 70 million people would be dead,' a drunk Nixon once declared at a dinner party, before deciding to stay put and drink a bit more.

One near-victim was apparently Cambodia, a country that the Viet Cong occasionally used as a hideout during the height of the Vietnam War. When this fact came up in conversation during a drink-sodden summer holiday, it's said that the less-than-sober president flew into a rage. 'He just got pissed,' a secret service agent later reported. 'They were half in the tank, sitting around the pool drinking. And Nixon got on the phone and said: "Bomb the shit out of them!"'

Fortunately, his orders were ignored – but when it came to North Korea, it was a close-run thing. After that Soviet ally shot down a US spy plane, 'Nixon became incensed and ordered a tactical nuclear strike,' according to the CIA's George Carver. 'The joint chiefs were alerted and asked to recommend targets, but Kissinger got on the phone to them. They agreed not to do anything until Nixon sobered up in the morning.'

And (while it certainly got more than its fair share of Napalm), Vietnam can at least be thankful that it didn't also get nuked. 'Nixon was drunk and he said, "Henry, we've got to nuke them,"' according to a Kissinger aide.

Thankfully, Kissinger said 'no'. As Nixon became 'increasingly incapable of playing his role as the leader of the free world,' his secretary of state 'gained an imperial power over foreign policy'. 'There were many times when a cable would come in late and Henry would say, 'There's no sense waking him up – he's incoherent.'

But enough of all this. In all fairness, we should note that Nixon's problems weren't all brought on by drinking. He also enjoyed popping pills.

Shortly after winning the presidency, the president who famously began the West's 'war on drugs' was given a few thousand Dilantins by a (non-doctor) friend. Handing over medicine that's generally used to treat seizures, Nixon's pal was convinced that they'd also cure his anxiety.

Subsequent research has shown that Dilantin can indeed reduce anxiety ... when it's taken in small doses for short periods of time, and not mixed with other medicines or alcohol. But it's also been shown cause 'mental confusion, dizziness, insomnia (and) transient nervousness' in people who don't meet those conditions. And let's just say that, along with sleeping pills, Dicky took two a day.

'If such a user of the drug were the president of the United States,' says Dr Lawrence McDonald, 'I would be very nervous. Mental confusion is not something you want in a leader. Dilantin certainly could impair someone of that calibre from making correct and timely and appropriate judgments. It's a potential time bomb.'

Or, indeed, a potential nuke.

THE WORLD'S STRONGEST DRINKS

If drinks were weapons, these would be nuclear.

- Balkan Vodka (Serbia, 88 per cent)
- River Antoine Royale Grenadian Rum (Grenada, 90 per cent)
- Bruichladdich X4 Quadrupled Whiskey (Scotland, 92 per cent)
- Everclear (USA, 95 per cent)
- Spirytus (Poland, 96 per cent)

BIG SIPS SINK SHIPS

Did alcohol help sink the Titanic?

'If you drink, don't drive. Don't even putt.'
                                                Dean Martin

Don't drink and drive, TV ads often tell us, but they should probably add that we should not drink and *sail*. Just as 'loose lips sink ships', according to the World War II slogan, history shows us that wet lips can too. The past century is full of sea captains who had a few drinks too many and were busy having another one when their ship started to sink.

Could the *Titanic*'s captain have fallen into this category? At least one survivor certainly thought so. 'The boat struck an iceberg at 11 o'clock on Sunday night,' Emily Richards wrote in a letter to a relative a week or two after her rescue. 'The Captain was down in the saloon drinking and gave charge to someone else to steer the ship. It was the Captain's fault.'

So did she actually *see* this, or was she just reporting a rumour? We'll never know for certain, as Captain Smith rather heroically chose to go down with his ship.

The captain of the *Costa Concordia*, however, was perhaps a touch less heroic when that Italian cruise ship struck a rock in 2012. Thirty-three lives were lost during the chaotic six-hour evacuation, but you'll be glad to know that his wasn't one of them. 'I was trying to get people to get into the boats in an orderly fashion,' Captain Schettino later explained to the press, when they asked why he'd abandoned the ship within seconds, leaving hundreds of passengers still stranded on board. 'Suddenly, since the ship was at a 60 to 70 degree angle, I tripped and I ended up in one of the boats. That's how I found myself there.'

All this sounds a little implausible to me. Particularly as, once ashore, he refused to obey the coast guard's order to return to his command, instead requesting a pair of dry socks.

But let's not be too quick to judge. In Schettino's defence, he was said to have been drunk at the time, not to mention high on cocaine. According to one of his officers the *Costa Concordia* had hit the submerged rock because Schettino had been 'driving it like a Ferrari' – and in shallow waters where it was not supposed to go. He had done so in order to sail by and 'salute' a small island, hoping to impress the passengers and a fellow crewmember whose family lived there.

Still, at least the rock he hit was *submerged*. It's not like Schettino crashed into something big and obvious like, say, Britain. But it would seem that one Russian ship managed to do just that, after the sailor that was placed in charge of the lookout managed to work his way through a full litre of rum. A 7000-tonne cargo ship that was over 120-metres long, *Lyblinsk Seaways* was going full speed one fateful night in 2015 when it suddenly slammed into the west coast of Scotland. 'Empty beer, wine and spirit bottles and cartons found on board after the accident indicated significant levels of alcohol consumption by the crew,' journalists later reported, while the night watchman was still eight times over the legal limit in a test taken a day after the crash.

That particular disaster resulted in 25 tonnes of oil being leaked into the sea – which, as maritime disasters go, is actually pretty small fry. For environmental destruction on a truly grand scale, I give you the *Exxon Valdez*. One of the most remote and inaccessible places on the planet, the clear blue waters of Alaska's Prince William Sound used to be 'a pristine vision of untouched beauty'. But that was before a 180,000-tonne oil tanker turned up in 1989 and started to make its way through a 16-kilometre-wide shipping channel.

You might think that 16 kilometres makes for a reasonably wide channel, and according to the coastguard you'd be entirely correct. 'This was not a treacherous area,' Commandant Yost told journalists after the 'almost unbelievable' accident. 'Your children could drive a tanker through it.'

But I'm guessing that your children aren't usually drunk. When the *Exxon Valdez* somehow managed to crash into one side of the channel, it was sailing under the command of one Captain Hazelwood, who at the time was said to have been snug and warm below deck, sleeping off a rather big bender.

But at least he was in better shape than Prince William Sound. Around 10 million gallons of crude oil was spilled into its clear blue waters that day, turning them a sort of sludgy poo-brown. Up to a quarter of a million seabirds died as a result, along with thousands of sea otters, hundreds of harbor seals, several orcas and innumerable fish.

Drink, sail, bloody idiot. Or, if you prefer: don't booze and cruise.

THE ALCOHOL ADVANTAGE

In sporting (as opposed to social) settings, we generally think of alcohol as an inhibitor to good performance. Not too many athletes head to the track after a couple of G&Ts or a big swig from a bottle of Jaeger. But in professional shooting, strange to say, a moderate amount of alcohol is actually considered a performance-enhancing drug, because it slows your heart rate just enough to aid concentration. This might help to explain why darts and pool are such popular pub sports, and why so many of us tend to play better – or at least a bit less badly – after a quick drink or two.

GREAT AUSTRALIAN PISS-UPS

Sir Edmund Barton, 1897

'When in Brisbane about a year ago, you got so disgracefully drunk and incapable that medical aid had to be called in so that you could be "toned up" in time to address a big public meeting. On that occasion, your condition and demeanour, the result of your drinking, so shocked some of the audience nearest the platform that they left in shame and disgust ... I charge you with being very frequently under the influence of drink .... when you were supposed to be discharging the duties of your high constitutional office of Prime Minister.

'Quite recently, you came into chamber so drunk you were scarcely able to stand, while on another occasion, seeing your drunken, helpless state, the Speaker generously put an end to the painful scene [when] he saw you were incapable of properly doing [so] ...'

Labor journalist and politician John Norton in an 'open letter' to Australia's first prime minister.

Sir John Kerr, 1977

'His obvious inebriation, combined with his thicket of white hair and his aristocratic bearing, made him seem more like a Barry Humphries' character than the governor general.'

Journalist Jacqueline Maley on the time Australia's governor general presented the Melbourne Cup.

John Howard, 1990

'I had a couple of South Australian reds. I remember that night, yes. I can't dispute the story.'

Yet another former PM on the time he attended Parliament in less than peak condition.

Kevin Rudd, 2007

'I saw a couple of stories about people grabbing, touching dancers – nobody in the party grabbed anybody. Nobody was thrown out of the place, they ordered a round of beers and the Australian guys acted like gentlemen.

'He didn't even have time to drink [the beer] he just said, "Oh no, this won't do". Cos you're looking at the screen and you just see like a soccer game or a boxing match, and all of a sudden a girl's taking off her dress, and he's like. "Oh no, this won't do."

'It was really nothing big, I don't know why everyone's making a big thing out of this, I didn't realise this guy was anyone important.'

The owner of a New York strip club after the former Australian prime minister paid his establishment a visit.

Tony Abbott, 2013

'I think quite a few bottles of wine were consumed by the three of us. I think all of us were in a mellow and reflective mood, so the reflections went on for longer and later than they should have and the impact was rather greater than it should have been ... I lay down and next thing I knew it was morning.'

The former prime minster on the day he went missing in Parliament.

DRUNKEN DICTATORS

Why despots should steer clear of drinks

> 'It is most absurdly said, in popular language, of any man, that he is disguised in liquor; for, on the contrary, most men are disguised by sobriety.'
>
> — Thomas de Quincy

We all waste money from time to time. I myself once bought a gym membership.

But that's nothing compared to Kim Jong Un. The Supreme Leader of North Korea is thought to spend something like US$645 million a year on the worthy cause that is Kim Jong Un. From flashy cars and caviar, to private theatres and one-man ski resorts, his lifestyle is arguably a touch extravagant when you consider how his subjects are kind of starving.

But it would be a mistake to think that Kim is a man who has everything. Even a Supreme Leader must sometimes miss out. I am, of course, talking about North Korea's failure (to date) to develop any really state-of-the-art military satellites. This has long been an issue for the Ever-Victorious, Iron-Willed Commander, to use another one of his official titles – and when he got drunk at a banquet in 2016, it became an issue for some of his generals as well. Calling them 'traitors of the nation' for their failure to develop said satellites, the Father of the People ordered them to stay up all night writing letters of apology, on pain of death – letters of apology that he was somewhat puzzled to receive the next morning when he woke up remembering nothing. Exhausted, relieved and ink-stained, it's said that North Korea's most high-ranking generals immediately broke down and started to cry.

Just another day in the life of the Bright Sun of the 21st Century, a puffy-faced rumoured alcoholic who is said to spend close to a million a year on cognac and once drank ten bottles of Bordeaux in a single meal. Kim's most famous feat while off his face was ordering the execution of two of his uncle's aides. He was 'very drunk' a source later said.

The moral of this story is that when a dictator is drunk, you should probably look for the door. Though this would not have been news to anyone near Caligula, a Roman emperor who loved a tipple – when he wasn't murdering his siblings or shagging his sister. Or torturing, killing, enslaving or raping pretty much everyone else. Eventually assassinated by one of his servants (who stabbed him a somewhat superfluous 30 times), Caligula's drink-sodden approach to government was best illustrated by a time in 39 CE when he ordered that a floating bridge be built off the coast of Naples for, well, no reason at all. Stretching over three kilometres, and made of hundreds of boats tied together and covered in planks, the completion of this utterly pointless bridge was considered cause for a party. So Caligula promptly organised one, and invited several local citizens aboard. They got to stand around and see him get shitfaced, then decide that it might be fun to ride along the bridge on a big golden chariot pulled by a big team of racehorses. And then they got to be knocked into the ocean … and made to stay there until they all drowned.

Not what you'd call the most fun party ever. Though I have to say that I've been to worse.

Anyway, dying at the hands of a drunk at least meant that his guests didn't live to see Nero, another Roman emperor who liked a sip. *His* idea of a party, it's said, involved smearing Christians with tar and having them tied to wooden stakes on a grassy plain just outside of his palace. Nero's equally drunk guests would then gather beside a window and watch each of these God-botherers get set alight, and oh-so-slowly turn into small piles of ash. Supposedly responsible for murdering his mum, Nero is also said to have kicked his pregnant wife to death in the midst of a drunken rage. He was a bit down about it the next day, of course, but soon cheered up when one of his servants found him a slave boy who looked a bit like the former Mrs Nero. Legend says that Nero had the boy castrated and dressed up like his dead wife in a drunk effort to honour her.

Such could be life for slaves, unfortunately. And not just in Rome, but in China too. The far-east's most far-out leader, as far as drinking was concerned, was Wenxuan of Northern Qi, an emperor whose alcoholism was said to lead him into terrible rages, and was certainly bad news for his prisoners. The story goes that he liked to have a group of them brought to his chambers every evening so that he could kill someone, should the urge take him after a few drinks.

Though, to be fair, Wenxuan wasn't just a drunken murderer. Drunken rape was another one of his hobbies. He had a habit, whatever the weather, of stripping down and running about demanding sex from any woman who caught his eye, and killing her if she refused.

But even acquiescence was no guarantee of safety. On one famous (and, needless to say, drunken) occasion, Wenxuan discovered that one of his 'conquests' had had sex with someone else a couple of years previously – and what's worse, that that someone else was his cousin. Consumed with jealousy, he immediately ordered said cousin to kill himself, and swiftly had his conquest's head chopped off. He then took her body to a banquet, cut it into pieces and started playing with her leg in front of his rather unsettled guests. Afterwards he packed her body into a cart and followed it around on foot, crying the whole time.

Which is kind of sweet, if you take the big, broad view. The course of true love never did run smooth.

Anyway, Attila the Hun might have appreciated it, at least. Though his enemies knew him as 'a savage destroyer' and the 'Scourge of God,' that barbarian did have a romantic side. For evidence, I give you one of his wedding nights (he was a man who had multiple wives). Supposedly pleased with his latest acquisition, a no-doubt terrified blonde with the name of Ildico, Attila got blind drunk at the banquet, then dragged her upstairs for some tender love-making. But he never came back down. Passed out on the bed, the Scourge of God got a severe nosebleed and choked to death in a drunken stupor.

Bad news for his Empire, but you'd have to suspect that Ildico was not ill-pleased.

MIND-BENDERS

Mushrooms, plants & LSD

The 18th of April 1943 started out just like any other day for a Swiss chemist called Albert Hofmann. Since he was at a laboratory researching 'scilla glycosides' and all of that sort of thing, this probably means that it started out dull. Don't get me wrong, I'm glad that the world has lots of scientists. But I'm even more glad that I am not one of them.

The point is that Hofmann's day eventually picked up. That afternoon, more or less on a whim, the 37-year-old decided to revisit an equally dull project that he'd abandoned five years ago: synthesising a chemical compound from a fungus called 'ergot', with a view to making some sort of medicine. So he fished out the fungus, started synthesising again – and in the process, got some stuff on his finger, which he absent-mindedly put in his mouth.

How do we know this? Because of what happened next. Finding himself 'affected by a remarkable restlessness, combined with a slight dizziness', the chemist decided to stop work and make his way home. Once there, Hofmann later recalled, he 'lay down and sank into a not unpleasant intoxicated-like condition, characterised by an extremely stimulated imagination. In a dreamlike state, with eyes closed (I found the daylight to be unpleasantly glaring), I perceived an uninterrupted stream of fantastic pictures, extraordinary shapes with intense, kaleidoscopic play of colours.'

'After about two hours, however, this condition faded away.'

So the next day, he naturally had a bit more.

'Little by little I could begin to enjoy the unprecedented colours and plays of shapes that persisted behind my closed eyes. Kaleidoscopic, fantastic images surged in on me, alternating, variegated, opening and then closing themselves in circles and spirals, exploding in coloured fountains, rearranging and hybridising themselves in constant flux ...'

What Hofmann had accidentally discovered was, of course, 'lysergsäure-diäthylamid' – a German phrase meaning 'lysergic acid', better known as 'LSD'. He had discovered a drug that could bend reality out of shape, then paint it orange and add a two-headed squirrel.

And it was a discovery that did not go unnoticed. Acid trips were embraced by psychiatrists and therapists in the 1950s, with Cary Grant just one of many patients to take LSD dozens of times. The CIA conducted all sorts of experiments as part of a ten-year program called MKUltra to develop mind control, and for all we know might be conducting them still. Above all, LSD became part of the counterculture – a way for '60s kids to turn on, tune in and drop out.

But acid wasn't really a 'discovery' at all. Sure, synthetic hallucinogens were born on that fateful day with Dr Hofmann, but in their natural form, they've been around forever. There are hundreds of psychoactive plants and herbs all over the world, and still more kinds of hallucinogenic mushrooms.

And the evidence suggests that our ancestors all knew this – that people have been turning on, tuning in and dropping out for thousands of years. 'It is generally thought that mind-altering substances, or at least drugs, are a modern-day issue, but if we look at the archaeological record, there are many data supporting their consumption in prehistoric times,' says Dr Elisa Guerra-Doce, whose research encompasses Europe, Asia and the Americas. 'As soon as drug plants and fermented drinks were first consumed, there is uninterrupted evidence for such use over centuries.'

And is there any evidence for that use affecting human history?

Gentle reader, it's time to find out.

Early evidence of hallucinogens

- c. 50,000 BCE – Neanderthal burial site in Iraq contains remains of the herbal stimulant ephedra
- c. 10,000 BCE – Evidence of earliest crops found in various locations, including psychoactive plants such as mandrake and cannabis
- c. 8600–5600 BCE – Fossilised remains of a hallucinogenic cactus found in Peru
- c. 7000–1000 BCE – Seeds of mescal beans found in various digs around Texas and Mexico
- c. 1000 BCE – 'Mushroom stones' found around Central America suggest hallucinogenic mushrooms used in sacred cults

European hallucinogens

- Fly agaric (mushroom)
- Ergo (fungus)
- Henbane (plant)*
- Mandrake (plant)*
- Hemlock (plant)*
- Belladonna (plant)*
*used in witches' brews

American hallucinogens

- Coca (plant)
- Jimsonweed (plant)
- Datura (plant)*
- Ayahuasca (plant)
- Salvia divinorum (plant)
- Peyote (cactus)
*used in witches' brews

Asian hallucinogens

- Opium poppy (plant)
- Betel nut (seed)

African hallucinogens

- Kwashi (plant)
- Iboga (plant)

Nicknames for LSD

- Acid
- Trips
- Tabs
- Gel
- Dots

Acid pros

- Euphoria
- Sense of relaxation
- Sense of well-being

Acid cons

- Hallucinations
- Anxiety/paranoia and feelings of panic
- Dizziness
- Blurred vision
- Irregular heartbeat
- Palpitations

Acid big-time cons

- Depression
- Psychosis
- Gastric bleeding
- Coma

ART FOR ART'S SAKE?

Did hallucinogenic drugs help create art?

> 'Psilocybin actually changes one domain of personality that is strongly related to traits such as imagination, feeling, abstract ideas and aesthetics, and is considered a core construct underlying creativity in general ... And the changes we see appear to be long-term.'
>
> Dr Roland R Griffiths

Every time the government passes a budget, you can pretty much guarantee that some actor, writer, painter or musician will appear in the news and insist that they haven't spent enough on the arts. Governments can *never* spend enough on the arts, according to some of these folks: the public can never have enough unread poems or unattended plays or important movies that are also unwatchable.

And the thing is, they're probably right. As Haldane McFall rather pretentiously put it, 'That man who is without the arts is little above the beasts of the field.' Whether or not creating artsy stuff for the sake of it really is what makes us human, it certainly seems to be part of the equation.

I mean, think about it for a moment. What else is there that's uniquely 'human'? What's the actual, qualitative difference between some NRL players and a hairy creature you might find at the zoo? Chimpanzees are known to use tools, after all. And plenty of other animals are clearly able to co-operate, and form societies with complex ranks and roles. Lots of species have a language of sorts, and show an ability to reason, argue and empathise. Things like lying and showing off are not unknown among primates, and it's pretty clear that they can be status-conscious. And anyone who has ever owned a pet would know that they're capable of empathy and other 'human' emotions like jealousy and love.

But here's the thing. No other animal, to the best of our knowledge, does anything that one could really call 'art'. The closest thing to it that zoologists can find are those colourful little nests made by male bower birds. But they're not so much 'art for art's sake' as a way to woo chicks: like their human counterparts, female bower birds are turned on by a happening pad.

Creating an aesthetically pleasing object for no other reason than aesthetic pleasure seems to be a uniquely human practice. So when precisely did it begin?

Up until the 1970s, we thought that the answer was about 40,000 years ago – that being the approximate age of some statues found in a cave in Germany. But archaeologists have since discovered a few suggestive artefacts in the southern tip of Africa, such as a piece of ochre with geometric engravings that is thought to be at least 70,000 years old.

Either way, then, it's clear that art is quite old. But what's equally clear is that it's not as old as it could be – that it took quite a while to arrive. Homo sapiens have been around for 200,000 years, after all. It would seem that when we weren't hunting, gathering, sleeping and shagging, we spent about 130,000 years twiddling our thumbs.

So what changed? What inspired the first human to get out some charcoal, mix it with ochre, and smear something pretty on the wall of a cave? As Graham Hancock puts it, 'It is simply impossible to overstate the uniqueness and peculiarity of the evolutionary event by which we were drawn into fully modern consciousness.'

For other academics, it's also impossible to overstate its *importance*. Since a picture of, say, a horse, involves an ability to understand and use symbols (an ability that other animals seem to more or less lack), they say that this sudden aesthetic impulse may actually have been a major step towards modern human cognition. Cave art, in other words, was not just an 'effect' of human braininess, but also, in some way, its cause.

Anyway, I'll tell you what's *not* impossible: the notion that these first artworks were inspired by drugs. Professors Tom Froese, Alexander Woodward and Takashi Ikegami published an analysis of prehistoric paintings from all over the globe, and found that most of them have a great deal in common. Particular types of 'spiral-like and labyrinthine designs' pop up again and again in caves that are separated by thousands of miles.

And where *else* do these sorts of images tend to pop up? In a human brain that's on hallucinogenic drugs. Technically known as 'Turing instabilities', these weirdly consistent geometric designs mimic the structural makeup of the brain when the person who owns said brain is having a good time. 'When these visual patterns are seen during altered states of consciousness,' the researchers argue, 'they are directly experienced as highly charged with significance. In other words, the patterns are directly perceived as somehow meaningful and thereby offer themselves as salient motifs for use in rituals.'

What they're saying here is that all these swirly-whirly, tie-dye-like hippie squiggles didn't keep recurring in caves through some kind of ancient coincidence. They kept popping up because, just like many an artist today, a lot of ancient artists liked to get high. 'The prevalence of certain geometric patterns in the symbolic material culture of many prehistoric cultures, starting shortly after the emergence of our biological species and continuing in some indigenous cultures until today, is explained in terms of the characteristic contents of biologically determined hallucinatory experience.'

Want that in English? Well, essentially what they're saying is that cave art was a ritual of sorts: people would swallow a psychedelic plant, start to feel a bit funny, and then try to express that funny feeling with paint on a wall.

If true, then drugs are ultimately what gave us da Vinci. Though on the other hand, they also gave us Ken Done.

THE ART OF GETTING HIGH

Plenty of high-profile artists are rumoured to have had major drug habits, including Australia's own Brett Whitely (heroin), Andy Warhol (cocaine) and even Pablo Picasso (marijuana). But you'd be hard-put to find one who went to the lengths of contemporary artist Bryan Lewis Saunders. Saunders's most famous project has involved taking different drugs and creating self-portraits under their influence. His substances of choice have included prescription drugs such as Adderall and Oxycodone, recreational drugs from marijuana to crystal meth, and even makeshift drugs such as cough syrup (two bottles) and inhaling from a computer duster.

The resulting art varies wildly in style, but Saunders's experiment hasn't all been smooth. At the beginning he was trying a new drug each day, and reported that after a few weeks he 'became lethargic and suffered mild brain damage'. He's still going ahead with the experiment, but with bigger gaps between paintings, and only using drugs prescribed by his doctor.

THE HIGH OF THE BEHOLDER

Did hallucinogens help create religion?

'We have drunk Soma and become immortal; we have attained the light.'

The Rigveda

During the 1960s, a Harvard divinity student named Walter Pahnke conducted a fascinating experiment under controversial psychologist Timothy Leary. He gathered together a range of divinity students just before a Good Friday service and gave half the subjects a harmless vitamin pill. The rest were given an identical-looking pill that contained hallucinogens. Unaware of what they had taken, why they were there or what this experiment was supposed to achieve, said volunteers were then led to the chapel to pray, sing and sit through the service.

The next day, recovered, they all filled out a form about how they had felt at the time. Which, as you might imagine, was where things got interesting. It turned out that the volunteers who had taken the good stuff had a much more profound, mystical and moving afternoon in the stain-glassed House of Our Lord. And when they were surveyed some 25 years later, many described that same church service as an experience that had helped shape their life. 'It left me with a completely unquestioned certainty that there is an environment bigger than the one I'm conscious of,' said one such volunteer. 'I had my own interpretation of what that is, but it went from a theoretical proposition to an experiential one ... Somehow, my life has been different, knowing that there is something out there.'

What, if anything, can we take from this? How about the idea that drug use might have helped shape religion?

When you think about it, folks, is this *really* so controversial? Plenty of religious groups still use psychoactive plants, after all. The Rastafarians all smoke 'sacred' ganja, Native Americans worship with peyote, assorted hermetic sects employ LSD, and kava is still used in the Pacific when people want to get in touch with a god.

And this is because – when you get right down to it – the process of 'getting in touch with God' essentially involves getting in touch with your inner hippie. Regardless of the religion, or where, when or how it is practiced, all 'religious experiences' tend to involve the same sort of thing, which is simply some form of transcendence. Dancing, chanting, singing, drumming, swaying, praying and so forth. A spiritual moment just means switching your frontal lobes off and hanging out with the ones at the back.

All sorts of external elements can help us to do this, of course, which is why (much like nightclubs) churches tend to be big, grand and dark, with music, smoke and bright stained-glass windows. And fasting (in the manner of monks) can be a big help too.

But the easiest method is just to take a shitload of drugs – and it's probably the oldest one too. Hallucinogens are hardly an unusual find when archaeologists dig up ceremonial sites. Pre-colonial America, in particular, was practically a pharmacy. Be they Aztecs or Mayans or Toltecs or Mixtecs, pretty much every Mesoamerican nation that you've ever heard of seems to have accessed the spirit world through psychedelic plants. In Asia we can find cannabis seeds that date back dozens of centuries, while in Africa shamans eat what they call a 'dream root' just prior to delivering a prophecy.

What about the gods of the West? Well, it seems safe to assume that Zeus's daughter Helen had one or two dream roots of her own. After all, she gave the characters in the *Odyssey* 'a drug which eased men's pains and irritations and made them forget their troubles'. This drink 'would guarantee no man would let a tear fall on his cheek for one whole day, not even if his mother and his father died, or ... men armed with swords hacked down his brother or his son as he looked on'.

But let's face it, Zeus & co aren't all that much chop these days. If you believe in *them* you may as well believe in the tooth fairy, or in John Farnham's retirement.

So what about *God* god, the big guy in the Bible? What were people on when they claimed they saw *him*?

According to Professor Benny Shanon, Moses was on acacia. Do you remember that bit in the Old Testament when the Lord suddenly appeared in a burning bush and suggested that he lead the Jews to the Promised Land? Well, Shanon speculates that said bush was an acacia tree, a plant whose leaves (when dried and smoked) can get you seriously high.

'It was either a supernatural cosmic event, which I don't believe, or a legend, which I don't believe either, or finally, and probably, an event that joined Moses and the people of Israel under the effect of narcotics. I propose that this event involved no change in the real world, having nothing to do with either the bush or the fire. Rather, it is reflected in the radical alteration in the state of consciousness of the beholder – that is, Moses. Moses's sense of time changed and an actual moment in physical time was subjectively perceived as an eternity ... enough time for the bush in front of him to be burned and consumed. But in the external physical domain, only a fraction of a second had elapsed, hence no actual change in the bush was perceived.'

Interesting stuff from Professor Shanon – but, to my mind, also pretty speculative. For all we know Moses may not even have existed, which would have made getting high a bit of a challenge. Rather more interesting, I'd say, when you look at the Bible, is the fact that a lot of the stories in it seem to come from elsewhere. Predating the good book by hundreds of years are three other books that closely resemble it.

One of them is the *Rigveda*, a sacred text still revered by Hindus. It contains all sorts of echoes of the (not so) Old and New Testaments, from Adam and Eve and the Garden of Eden, all the way to ~~Krishna's~~ Jesus's birth, life and death. But what it *also* contains are repeated mentions of 'soma', a drink that it calls 'the Creator of the Gods' and says is made from the juice of a plant.

Probably it's the same drink that's discussed in the *Epic of Gilgamesh*, the also-pre-bible book from what's now Iraq. It's from *Gilgamesh* that we probably get the story of Noah's flood and pretty much everything that happens in Ecclesiastes. And in Gilgamesh you can also read about 'a plant that looks like a box-thorn', which lets you 'be again as you were in your youth'. 'This plant, Ur-shanabi, is the "Plant of Heartbeat", with it a man can regain his vigour.'

And then we have the Zoroastrian texts – stuff written in what's now Iran from as far back as 600 BCE. They contain some of humanity's oldest known descriptions of a heaven, hell, angels and demons, and they probably gave the writers of the Bible big chunks of Isiah. These texts also mention a sacred plant whose 'wise' and 'righteous' juice provides 'insight'.

Exactly what these plants were, we'll never know for sure. But please get in touch with the author if you think there's one in your garden ...

MEANWHILE, IN AUSTRALIA

The search for Australia's own hallucinogen has been going pretty much as long as Europeans have lived here. Many of those who came to the Great Southern Land just couldn't wait to find evidence that Indigenous religious ceremonies involved some sort of special plant. This search has been completely fruitless so far – and completely vegetable-less too.

Having said that, there have been claims over the centuries that some Indigenous tribes avoided eating certain kinds of mushrooms because they contained 'evil magic' or a connection to spirits. The bush tobacco called 'pituri' that's chewed by tribes across the continent was also a focus of study for years. In the 1870s, one scientist even injected it into a cat and a puppy hoping to see the poor animals trip out. Both creatures died almost straight away, without expressing any desire to dance or listen to a song by Bob Marley. Later, somewhat more scientific tests revealed that the plant's effects simply mirror tobacco's. On the scientific up-side, this means that Australians were probably the world's first people to discover the joys of nicotine.

DAVID VS THE DEVIL'S EYES

Did drugs make the Philistines philistines?

> *'I hate to advocate drugs, alcohol, violence, or insanity to anyone, but they've always worked for me.'*
>
> Hunter S Thompson

I'm not one of those geopolitical-relations-type experts that CNN turns to for insightful comments on the news. When something bad happens in Darfur, my response is to wonder where the hell Darfur is, and the same tends to go for trouble and strife in Kashmir.

I *can*, however, inform you with a certain degree of smug confidence that Palestinians and Israelis don't really get on. In fact, one might almost say that relations are tense; that in the atmosphere between them, there's a certain amount of chilliness. You might even go so far as to say a faint hint of frost.

Impressed, CNN? Yes, me too. And guess what, I can tell you still more. This slight tension is something that goes back a long way ... if the Palestinians are in any way related to the Philistines of the Bible.

Best known for giving us Goliath, and Samson's wily she-witch Delilah, the Philistines were a real-life people from no one-really-knows-where who arrived in what's now Israel during the Bronze Age. They gave their name to the place that we now call Palestine, and they gave the Israelites who lived nearby the shits. The Bible is full of uncomplimentary references to these apparently warlike people, who always seemed to be ruffling Israeli feathers in strangely named places like Eben-Ezer and Michmash.

'When Saul saw the army of the Philistines, he was afraid, and his heart trembled greatly,' we are told in 1 Samuel 28:5. And you can pretty much understand Saul's point of view, given that when these people had 'fought against Israel' in the past, 'the men of Israel [had] fled before the Philistines and fell slain on Mount Gilboa'. These were people you did not want to mess with. For hundreds of years, Goliath & co 'devoured Israel with an open mouth'. It's no coincidence that, in modern parlance, the word 'philistine' can mean oafish and violent.

There may well be some pot calling the kettle oafish and violent here, of course. The Israelites probably weren't great neighbours themselves, we just don't have a Philistine bible to tell us so. But while these mysterious people left no written records, they did leave behind a sprinkling of pots. Recently unearthed in an incineration pit near Tel Yavneh, a close examination of said pots has found tiny traces of a plant that looks a lot like henbane. Deadly in large doses, henbane is not something you'd eat for the purpose of nutrition, and it certainly doesn't have a nice taste. But you could eat it if you were keen to hallucinate.

'It's an old plant, and it has been documented in literature that Bedouin often chew it, to this day,' says Hebrew University researcher Dr Devori Mandar. 'The common presumption is that [the plants] served as an important part of mystic and spiritual rituals, and gave users intense, ecstatic experiences.'

Which sounds perfectly plausible – but what if it also did more? Suggestively nicknamed 'the devil's eyes', henbane has never been popular amongst hippy dippy types because of the way it can make users violent. 'This herb is called "insana wood",' a Dr Bartolomaeus announced way back in 1398, 'for the use thereof is perilous. If it be eate or dranke, it breedeth wodenes … and taketh away wytte and reason.'

'Wodenes', if you're wondering, means a mad, warlike fury (Woden being a warrior prone to going berserk). Could eating 'insana wood' before battle be what made what the Philistines so very terrifying? And, well, such philistines?

NO DRUGS, NO DEMOCRACY?

Does Western civilisation rest on hallucinogens?

'Then Helen, daughter of Zeus, took other counsel. Straightway she cast into the wine of which they were drinking a drug to quiet all pain and strife, and bring forgetfulness of every ill.'

Homer

It's pretty much impossible to avoid the phrase 'cradle of civilisation' when you are writing about ancient Greece. So I've decided, stuff it, I won't even try.

Yes, I'm well aware that 'civilisation' is an entirely subjective concept. And I realise that in Australia we generally use the word 'cot'. But it really does capture the way in which Greeks were being all urban and sophisticated at a time when pretty much everyone else was hitting people with clubs. In just a few short centuries during the Bronze Age, this busy little archipelago provided the foundations of Western politics and philosophy, and helped to create poetry and plays. Architecture and art also owe a lot to the Greeks, along with sport, sculpture and most of the sciences. And it's from the Greeks that we get words like 'logic,' 'dialogue,' 'sympathy' and 'democracy' – and you could say that they created the concepts too. The Greeks of the 4th and 5th century BCE gave us an unprecedented flowering of imagination and culture. They even gave us souvlaki and dips.

But what brought all this unprecedented flowering on, exactly? Why there? Why then? Why *them*?

Well, in some ways, you could say that Greek sophistication was a simple matter of geography. The ancient Greek states were based on a series of islands, and on a peninsula that was sealed off by mountains. Combined with their less-than-fertile and thus hard-to-farm soil, it was a set-up that discouraged would-be invaders – and forced the Greeks themselves to sail, build and trade. In other words, instead of spending all their lives with a spade or a sword, Greeks were better off using their brains. And the ideas and information that traders brought back to Greece gave those brains plenty to work with.

Still, is that the *whole* story? Because ancient lands like Carthage also sailed and traded a lot, and farmed very little, stranded as they were on the edge of the desert. But you didn't see too many Carthaginians strutting about in white togas celebrating the power of reason, and creating eternal works of literature and art. From all accounts they were too busy sacrificing children to the gods and turning people they didn't like into slaves.

If this story has another chapter, an underground temple that was recently unearthed in Epirus may provide a hint of its contents. Along with broken pots and tiles and all that sort of guff, the archaeologists who excavated it in the 1950s and '60s found something that was actually interesting: traces of beans and seeds that can cause hallucinations.

Why were they there? Well, for Dr Enrico Mattievich, the temple's 'dank halls' probably served as a sort of labyrinth of death, where ancient Greeks could go to get a taste of the afterlife. 'After a long stay in the dark and segregation, magic rites, prayers, invocations, wandering about mysterious halls, [and] a special diet [of hallucinogens], pilgrims reached the right mental and psychological state to be brought into contact with the dead.'

And that's far from the only evidence of drugs in Greek culture. A much bigger and better known one comes in the form of the Eleusinian Mysteries, a coming-of-age religious ceremony (not unlike a Bar Mitzvah) held just outside Athens every year. Pretty much anyone who was anyone in ancient Greece – from Aristotle and Sophocles to Plato and Diagorus – would make the solemn trek to the little town of Eleusis and participate in several days' worth of rites. They would bathe, pray and purify, recite texts and fast. And they would do other things that are, yes, a mystery.

But it's pretty clear that one of them was take drugs. A crucial rite involved drinking a sacred potion called the 'kykeon', which would deliver all sorts of mystical insights into the meaning of life. And it's clear that 'initiates' were never quite the same after slamming it down. 'Considered one of the peak experiences of initiates' lives', according to toxicologist Philip Wexler the drink was said to 'have a profound and life-changing impact' that forever 'affected their beliefs and behaviours'.

We'll never know what was in the kykeon, but it's hard to believe that it wasn't some sort of hallucinogen. Ergot – an LSD-like fungus that grows on grain – is one candidate, a theory made more likely by the fact that Demeter, the goddess of the grain harvest, was a big part of the ritual. But mushrooms or half a dozen other then-common plants would have done the job just as well.

One scholar, at least, has no doubts about it. The Greeks 'were drug users, plain and simple', says Dr David Hillman, author of *The Chemical Muse: Drug Use and the Roots of Western Civilization*. 'They grew the stuff, they sold the stuff ... from this world in which drugs were a universally accepted part of life sprang art, literature, science, and philosophy.'

Yes, as far as Hillman can see, the Greek philosophers whose ideas lead to the very first democracy were 'the biggest drug-using lunatics of them all ... much more like medicine men than philosophers'. And if he's right there, then it might just be fair to say that without drugs, there would be no democracy.

PSYCHEDELIC FISH

People being the incredibly creative creatures that they are (I exclude accountants and TV executives of course), it should come as no surprise that our search for drugs has extended well beyond plants and mushrooms. One of our most interesting discoveries is a species of sea bream called 'salema porgy' which those in the know like to call the 'dreamfish'. A recreational drug in Ancient Rome, it came back into the public eye in 2006 when two Mediterranean men accidentally ate some and wound up having a whale of a time.

THE DRUGGIE OF DELPHI

How getting high helped to tear down an empire

'Nitrous oxide and ether ... stimulate the mystical consciousness in an extraordinary degree. ... [In] the nitrous oxide trance we have a genuine metaphysical revelation. [Our] normal waking consciousness is but one special type of consciousness, whilst all about it, parted from it by the filmiest of screens, there lie potential forms of consciousness entirely different.'

Dr William James

Have you ever heard the phrase 'as rich as Croesus'? Well, it may not surprise you to learn that this Croesus fellow was pretty well off. Possibly the first ever monarch to use gold and silver to mint his own coins, Croesus ruled Lydia (in what's now Turkey) about 2500 years ago – but after a while, he decided he wanted to rule even more. Wildly wealthy, he built the Temple of Artemis, one of the seven wonders of the world, with some of his spare change, and used the rest to build up a great army.

His next step was to go off to the Delphi to ask the oracle if it was a good time to wage war. Delphi, if you don't know, was a big shrine on the slopes of Mount Parnassus, near Greece's Gulf of Corinth. Chockful of statues and monuments and temples and treasures, it was in many ways the centre of the ancient Greek world, attracting visitors from every part of the Mediterranean and from states, empires and kingdoms beyond. Philosophers, statesmen, monarchs, merchants: all tried to go to Delphi at least once in their life, and so too did ordinary farmers and fishermen.

But they didn't just come to see statues; what they wanted to see was the future. Delphi was a big deal because it was the home of the oracle: a well-born woman who sat in a temple and told prophecies to her constant stream of visitors. Whenever the oracle died of old age, she'd be replaced by another one – and then would come another one, and another one after that. For over a millennium, the Oracle of Delphi advised everyone from Solon and Socrates to Alexander the Great. Though, prone as she was to being incoherent and vague, 'advised' may be too generous a term.

Take Croesus for example. 'Shall I invade Persia,' that monarch asked the oracle (having already presented her with a gigantic lion statue made out of pure gold).

'If you send an army against the Persians,' she duly replied, 'a great empire shall be destroyed.'

So invade and destroy a great empire Croesus duly did. But it turned out that 'the great empire' that got destroyed was his own. Amid the smoking ruins of his army, the once mighty king was taken prisoner and sentenced to be burned at the pyre.

The moral of this story is generally said to be 'don't over-reach', but I'd say that the real moral is 'don't trust a druggie'. For over 1000 years, visitors to Delphi made all sorts of important life decisions – they married, they migrated, they meddled, they murdered – on the advice of some random chick who was completely off her chops.

What do I mean, precisely? Plutarch provides the clue. That ancient essayist wasn't always an ancient essayist: early on in his career, he was a Delphic priest. Plutarch later reported that the oracle needed to get into a sort of trance before she could ever have a vision, and that this trance only ever came on after she spent time in a particular room. The room was a small underground chamber at the bottom of the temple ... that was saturated with sweet-smelling fumes.

Thousands of years later, geologists claimed to have discovered the source of said fumes: the temple was built on the intersection of two little cracks in the Earth's crust. The earthquakes to which Greece is prone continually rattle these cracks, making the ground much more permeable and full of tiny little crevices through which hallucinogenic gases can rise. Dr Jelle De Boer even found evidence of one such gas in a nearby spring: ethylene, which 'has a sweet smell and produces a narcotic effect described as a floating or disembodied euphoria'. 'Plutarch made the right observation,' he writes. 'Indeed, there were gases that came through the fractures.'

'Ethylene inhalation is a serious contender for explaining the trance and behaviour of the Pythia,' agrees Professor Diane Harris-Cline. 'Combined with social expectations' – not to mention low levels of oxygen – 'a woman in a confined space could be induced to spout off oracles.'

And a king with confined IQ could be induced to listen to them.

MEANWHILE, IN AUSTRALIA

The 1960s and '70s in Australia weren't just a time of peace and love and bright velvet pants. They were also a time of terrifying, LSD-fuelled yoga cults. Or at least *a* terrifying, LSD-fuelled yoga cult. Our very own druggie religion went by the name of 'The Family', a group led by a yoga teacher named Anne Hamilton-Byrne that operated in the outskirts of Melbourne. A 'hotch-potch' of Christianity and Eastern mysticism, The Family's beliefs were based on the idea that Hamilton-Byrne was the reincarnation of Jesus and a living god, and that her inner circle were her 'Apostles'.

The group's members were mostly middle-class professionals, and many of them came from the medical industry, specifically Newhaven Hospital in Kew. Their patients were frequently given LSD and recruited to the group, while current members would often take a trip to the hospital, and then take a trip while they were there.

Even more unpleasant was Hamilton-Byrne's habit of 'adopting' children, dyeing their hair blond and beating them, all while feeding them a vast range of drugs. One ritual involved giving a child LSD and then locking them in a dark room.

In 1987 the police got involved and took the children away, but thanks to a legal loophole or two the leaders got away with some fines. The Family still exists to this day.

GOING BESERK

Were all those Viking marauders on mushies?

'We were back at home, and I had returned to that reassuring but profoundly unsatisfactory state known as "being in one's right mind".'

Aldous Huxley

There's a lot to be said about Scandinavians, though not much of it occurs to me. Lovely people, I'm told – if a touch too fond of thrash metal. Sweden had some pretty handy tennis players back in the day and ... um ... I believe that Norwegians quite enjoy eating fish.

One thousand years ago, that introduction would have been a whole lot easier to write, even though I would have had to use a parchment and quill. Scandinavians back then weren't affluent, sensible, slightly colourless types with excellent welfare systems and cheap wooden furniture. One thousand years ago, Scandinavians were *Vikings*. Brutal, axe-swinging, fur-clad barbarians who raped and pillaged their way through Europe for the best part of three centuries, petrifying pretty much everyone within ten miles of a coast.

'Never before has such terror appeared in Britain as we have now suffered from a pagan race,' reported one such citizen after said barbarians plundered a monastery in Yorkshire. Deciding that it might be fun to kill a few monks while they were at it, 'the heathens poured out the blood of saints around the altar ... [and] trampled on the bodies ... like dung in the streets.'

Good times. Then, a few years later, it was Ireland's turn. 'The sea spewed forth floods of foreigners over Erin,' reads 820's *Annals of Ulster*, 'so that no haven, no landing-place, no stronghold, no fort and no castle might be found' that was not 'submerged by waves of Vikings and pirates'. Resistance was not so much useless as an extremely bad idea. This was because whenever a local *did* fight back, they risked what the Viking invaders liked to call a 'blood-eagle'. The ancient equivalent of a one-on-one dinner with Peter Dutton, in the words of historian Patrick Wormald it involved 'ripping a victim's lungs out of his ribcage and draping them across his shoulders like eagles' wings'.

Though, having said that, other monastic records describe a time when a bishop in Canterbury spoke in defence of his flock, and while the Vikings *there* 'became greatly incensed', they certainly didn't blood-eagle him. No, they just 'pelted him to death with bones and the heads of cattle' until 'his holy blood fell upon the earth'.

Nice. Or, rather, not nice. But let's at least give the horned ones their due. Vikings didn't just butcher women, children and the occasional monk – they also slaughtered regular soldiers. From their earliest atrocities, right up until their final 'orgy of violence', these sailors didn't just play it safe by raiding defenceless little villages, they also fought and won some full-scale pitched battles against much larger forces. From Russia and Turkey to Germany and France, the Vikings didn't just sail in, steal stuff and slip away in the night. They frequently stuck around, fought a big army and beat it. As Priit Vesilind put it in *National Geographic*, 'In a casually brutal age, Vikings were simply better brutes.'

But how? How did this relatively small group of (not actually all that big) men manage to subjugate such a big chunk of Europe? Burly, bearded, barbaric types lived all over the continent, after all; this was an era when executions were an outing for kids. What made the barbarians from Scandinavia so much more terrifying than the barbarians from everywhere else?

Well, it helped that they had the berserkers. A sort of an elite commando unit tasked with charging at the enemy and breaking their will with batshit-crazy savagery, these fearless shock troops were named for the bear skins (*ber-serkrs*) they wore into battle instead of armour or mail. The word 'berserk' comes from them, and that's because 'berserk' is exactly what these people were.

Mind you, they were only berserk before going into a battle. Perfectly normal people the rest of the time, these warriors would fall into a sort of crazy trance called a *berserkergang* when the time came to pick up their axes – a trance that somehow saw them lose all awareness of everyday things like fear, reason, pity and pain. 'A demoniacal frenzy suddenly took him,' is how one observer describes a berserker in the midst of a trance. 'He furiously bit and devoured the edges of his shield; he kept gulping down fiery coals; he snatched live embers in his mouth and let them pass down into his entrails; he rushed through the perils of crackling fires; and at last, when he had raved through every sort of madness, he turned his sword with raging hand against the hearts of six of his champions.'

'Neither fire nor iron told upon them,' is how another chronicler describes the typical berserker's performance in battle. Prone to growl, howl, shriek, bite and absent-mindedly slaughter their friends, berserkers were 'as mad as dogs', 'as strong as oxen', and able to 'kill at a blow'. Like the black knight in *Monty Python's Holy Grail*, no serious injury could stop a berserker from fighting – and then fighting and fighting some more. (Alternatively, think of Tony Abbott's constant refusal to quit politics.)

But eventually 'this condition ceased' – and when it did, a great 'dulling of the mind and feebleness' followed, which could last for several days.

Does any of this sound faintly familiar?

For centuries, it was presumed that a *berserkergang* simply involved being crazily drunk. But drunkenness is hardly unknown among soldiers, and would hardly ever have such a pronounced effect. It's now considered far more likely that they ate magic mushrooms – *Amanita muscaria* being far from uncommon in the frozen fjords.

DOUBLE, DOUBLE TOIL AND TROUBLE

Are drugs why witches ride broomsticks?

'If God dropped acid, would he see people?'
Steven Wright

Not all food is actually edible, as anyone who's been to Taco Bill knows. I once ate their chicken enchiladas, and let's just say that death is no longer something I fear.

But even that dish might be preferable, on balance, to the brew those witches make in *Macbeth*. Do you remember it? How they double, double toil and trouble by making a fire burn and a cauldron bubble? Well, eye of newt and toe of frog, wool of bat and tongue of dog are actually some of the tastier ingredients in that particular mix. Others include the nose of a Turk and the liver of a Jew, a dead baby's finger and a few shards of yew. Sure, it's not as bad as Taco Bill's Baja fish taco, but you must admit that it runs a very close second.

In real life, however, a witch's brew would have been quite a bit tastier – and quite possibly healthy as well. 'Witches' were simply 'wise women', after all, and their brews were just medieval medicine. Mostly made out of herbs, spices, resins and such like, 'magic potions' were just like the stuff you'd find in a pharmacy today: potions and salves to cure disease and dull pain. And just like stuff you find in a pharmacy, every now and then they would actually work.

But some potions may have done a little more than that. In the 16th century, some Spanish women accused of witchcraft were found to have been 'anointing themselves' with 'certain green unguent ... composed of herbs such as hemlock, nightshade, henbane and mandrake'.

All four herbs are seriously hallucinogenic, but why turn them into an ointment? The answer relates to why witches ride broomsticks, and I very much hope that it comes as a shock. Eating hemlock and nightshade can make you seriously ill, and if you throw in some henbane it can also make you seriously dead. Applied to certain areas of the skin, however, they will just make you feel pleasant and floaty ... and those certain areas of the skin are the vagina and rectum.

Which brings us to broomsticks and why witches 'ride' them ... Here's a quote from a 14th-century trial. 'In rifleing the closet of the ladie', some 'witch hunters' reported that they 'found a pipe of oyntment, wherewith she greased a staffe, upon which she ambled and galloped through thick and thin.'

And here's another quote from a century later. 'The vulgar believe, and the witches confess, that on certain days or nights they anoint a staff and ride on it to the appointed place or anoint themselves under the arms and in other hairy places.' Hopping 'on' a broomstick, in other words, was simply a great way to get high.

All right, then. What's next?

Oh, yes: Salem, Massachusetts. Immortalised in Arthur Miller's *The Crucible*, history's most famous instance of witching-hunting kicked off in the winter of 1692. What happened was that two little girls in the isolated little village suddenly started to suffer from a strange series of fits. They hallucinated, they ranted, they fell into long, blank-eyed trances. They complained of creepy, crawly sensations all over their skin. So the highly trained village doctor naturally announced that they'd fallen victim to witchcraft, then sat back and watched as accusations started to fly.

Within months, some 120 other 'witches' had been placed under arrest, and 19 had been hung from a noose. Several more villagers – not just girls – had fallen victim to 'demonic fits' in this time, but it had also become clear that the witchcraft didn't simply stop there. If a villager woke up feeling odd, got a rash or couldn't sleep, he would immediately conclude that some spell was to blame. The only question was which witch cast it.

Come spring, however, everybody suddenly calmed down. The frenzy of fits, accusations and counter-accusations rapidly fizzled out, and normal life more or less resumed. Community spirit probably wasn't what it had been, but – given these people were all dour, churchy Puritans – that wasn't necessarily such a bad thing.

So what the hell happened during that cold, crazy winter? The answer could well be ergot, a hallucinogenic fungus that can grow on rye bread. Eating bread baked with ergot-contaminated rye can have all sorts of unpleasant effects, including convulsions, delusions, creepy-crawly sensations on the skin, vomiting and hallucinations.

While the alkaloids in ergot are related to acid, you might call them the black sheep of the family. 'Unlike LSD, the effects produced by ergot are not potentially pleasant,' says Sarah Lohman. 'You don't have a good trip. You never have a good trip. It only produces an unpleasant altered state in which you're experiencing mania, delirium, paranoia [and] troubling visions ... You could [also] have things like convulsions, interrupted speech, vomiting, diarrhoea, and it can even cause gangrenous symptoms, you could lose limbs, and eventually it could kill you.'

Good times.

Ergot poisoning is thought to have been behind the 'dancing plagues' of medieval Europe – assorted documented instances of random peasants suddenly starting to dance, sway and gibber in the streets to the mystification of passers-by and (later) themselves.

We don't know for a *fact* that ergot was at work in Salem, but we *do* know that rye was Salem's main crop. We also know that the previous spring had been unusually warm and damp, creating perfect conditions for fungus to grow. And we know that the 'winter of madness' was also a winter of extreme coldness. In the absence of fresh fruit and vegetables, most villagers would have had to make do on mouldy old bread.

And we know that when winter finished, the fits finished with it.

DASHER AND DANCER

How exactly do Santa's reindeer get high?

> '[I experienced] a peculiar sense of wellbeing connected with the crazy sensation that my feet were growing lighter, expanding and breaking loose from my own body ... I experienced an intoxicating sensation of flying ... I soared where my hallucinations – the clouds, the lowering sky, herds of beasts, falling leaves ... billowing streamers of steam and rivers of molten metal – were swirling along.'
>
> Gustav Schenk

Did you know that there's a move in certain parts of Australia to ditch the phrase 'Merry Christmas' and replace with 'Happy Holidays'? The logic goes that it's more multicultural – that's it's a nice nod to all those Jews, Muslims, atheists and so on who don't happen to believe that the

Son of God was born on 25 December in a stable in Bethlehem, did something magic with loaves and fishes, cured a couple of lepers and then died for our sins.

As an atheist, I'd be okay with this policy. But as a pedant, I don't mind 'Merry Christmas'. Because however mono-cultural Yuletide may be in theory, in practice it's about as diverse as a day can get.

Want examples? Well, take the word 'Yuletide' itself. Once upon a time it described an annual festival that was celebrated by pagan German tribes: a festival that featured Yule logs and people singing songs door-to-door. Christmas trees and tinsel also originated in pre-Christian Germany, while wreaths and mistletoe were important symbols in and around ancient Greece.

There's more too: Christmas cake comes from Egypt, Christmas crackers come from France and Christmas cards apparently kicked off in England. Carols first emerged in 4th-century Rome, a place that – long before Jesus came along – had an annual holiday on 25 December to celebrate 'the birth of the sun'. Romans also celebrated the middle of winter by giving their friends and kids presents, though the origins of the Christmas stocking seem to owe more to Turkey's St Nicholas of Myra, a man who (along with the gift-giving, white-bearded Norse god Thor) was a model for Santa himself.

But what about all the reindeer? What about those eight magical animals that Santa straps to his sleigh and forces to fly all over the world in the space of a night? Where the hell did *they* come from?

Well, I'm sorry to say that Rudolf came from capitalism. In 1939, a Chicago department store was giving away colouring books as a Christmas promotion, and decided it would be cheaper to just produce their own.

Rudolf's chums pre-date him by over a century, but they come from America too. Dasher, Dancer, Donner, Blitzen & co all got their names from one Clement Clarke Moore, a poet whose most famous work appeared in New York's *Troy Sentinel* newspaper in 1823. (You think you don't know it, but actually you do. 'Twas the night before Christmas, when all through the house, not a creature was stirring, not even a mouse ... When what to my wondering eyes should appear, but a miniature sleigh, and eight tiny reindeer.')

But that's just their names. What about the fact that they're *flying reindeer*?! Did that whole thing begin with Moore too?

People generally say so. But something that you learn as you get older and wiser is that people are generally wrong. The first mention of flying reindeer predates Moore's poem by two years, and we can be pretty sure that said mention inspired it. 'Old Santeclaus with much delight, his reindeer drives this frosty night,' wrote an anonymous contributor to a book published by Moore's fellow New Yorker William Gilley. 'O'er chimney tops, and tracks of snow, to bring his yearly gifts to you.'

So where did this poet get the idea? Well, as Gilley explained to Moore's favourite paper, the *Troy Sentinel*, we'll never know, since 'the author of the tale but submitted the piece, with little added information'. 'However, it should be noted that he did mention the reindeer in a subsequent correspondence. He stated that far in the north near the Arctic lands a series of animals exist, these hooven and antlered animals resemble the reindeer and are feared and honoured by those around, as you see he claims to have heard they could fly from his mother. His mother being an Indian of the area.'

And here's where things get interesting. Because those Arctic lands – Scandinavia, Siberia and so forth – don't just contain big furry mammals with antlers who are quite good at pulling sleighs. They also contain hallucinogenic mushrooms called *amanita muscaria*, and an ancient tradition of scoffing them down. Several 18th- and 19th-century visitors to the region saw shamans and witch doctors use them to get into 'an exalted state' so as to be 'able to talk to the gods'.

Could the flying reindeer have something to do with this? 'At first glance, one thinks it's ridiculous, but it's not,' says Carl Ruck, a professor of classics at Boston University. 'Amongst the Siberian shamans, you have an animal spirit you can journey with in your vision quest. And reindeer are common and familiar to people in eastern Siberia.'

'Whoever heard of reindeer flying? I think it's becoming general knowledge that Santa is taking a "trip" with his reindeer.'

A merry Christmas indeed!

ANIMALS THAT TAKE HALLUCINOGENS

Reindeer themselves have been known to eat magic mushrooms now and then – and in nature, they're far from alone. While it's not always easy to tell why certain animals eat 'trippy' foods, and whether in fact they then trip at all, here are a handful of creatures that might just be enjoying life a bit more than they should.

- Koalas – Considering how little these marsupials move, it's no surprise their staple food, eucalyptus leaves, is known to have an intoxicating effect.

- Dolphins – Groups of dolphins have been recorded passing around an angry puffer fish, which releases a toxic chemical called 'tetrodotoxin'. The dolphins have then been spotted floating up near the surface of the water in a 'trance-like state'.

- Horses – Farmers are constantly trying to remove locoweed (which contains the chemical swainsonine) from their horse paddocks. Otherwise, the horses are known to get hooked on its effects, and their health seriously suffers as a result.

- Big-horned sheep – A rare hallucinogenic lichen can be found in the Canadian Rockies, and local sheep go to great lengths to taste it, rubbing the stuff into their teeth and gums to make sure they get every last bit.

- Capuchin monkeys – These monkeys have developed a strange habit of picking up poisonous millipedes and rubbing them all over their bodies. While it's suspected that the secretions help protect the monkeys against parasites, they also seem to enjoy the side-effect – that being, a blissful high.

BEYOND GOOD AND EVIL

Was Hitler's favourite philosopher entirely in his right mind?

'Reality is just a crutch for people who can't cope with drugs.'

Robin Williams

In 1934, a photograph appeared in the Nazi press of Adolf Hitler standing next to a statue. Taken during a visit to the Nietzsche archives – a sort of shrine to a then-long-dead thinker – the photo's caption read: 'the Führer before the bust of the German philosopher whose ideas have fertilised two great popular movements: the National Socialism of Germany and the Fascist movement of Italy.'

It's a caption that would have pleased Nietzche's sister, an ardent and outspoken anti-Semite, but would it have pleased the philosopher himself? Would he have been happy with the way his work came to be seen as consistent with fascism, and lend genocidal nutbags a whiff of cred?

The short answer is, who knows? Often called the 19th-century's most influential philosopher, Frederick Nietzsche was also its most incoherent. He's been claimed by conservatives, liberals, socialists, Marxists, anarchists and feminists, and praised by everyone from Sartre to Freud.

Having said that, Nietzsche also longed for a world that was 'beyond good and evil', a world that was run by 'noble races', not to mention a 'splendid blond beast'. He seemed to believe that most people are sheep who need to be governed by a wolf (or rather by a sort of 'superman' with the right 'will to power'). For Nietzsche, morality is 'a herd instinct' that holds people back. Most of us are just 'half-men' in need of a 'master'.

To fascists, of course, this was manna from heaven. Hitler adopted the phrase 'blond beast' and spoke of a 'master race', while it's said that Mussolini's 'reading of Nietzsche was one factor in converting him from Marxism to a philosophy of sacrifice and warlike deeds in defence of the fatherland'. 'Of all 19th-century thinkers, perhaps only Karl Marx has surpassed Nietzsche in his influence on the 20th century.'

But on the other hand, he also wrote stuff that those nutters would have liked less. Nietzsche denounced militarism, nationalism, racism and so on. Sure, he hated democracy, but he also seemed to hate everything else.

Essentially, it's hard to avoid the conclusion that what Nietzsche *really* hated was making sense. So he avoided it as much as possible. 'Whatever is profound, loves masks,' he once wrote, in one of those throwaway lines that could mean pretty much anything. Arguably he wasn't so much a philosopher as a slightly obscure and over-the-top poet.

And in the end, he became a mad one. The philosopher had a psychotic breakdown at age 44 after trying to stop a man whipping a horse. Mission accomplished, he apparently collapsed – convulsing – on the street, before returning to his boarding house where he danced about naked and threatened to go shoot the Kaiser. Despite occasional moments of lucidity, he spent the next decade in a vegetative state, eventually dying in a mental asylum, wholly unaware of his fast-growing fame.

It seems safe to suggest that this 'madness' didn't come out of the blue, and must have been present in some form when he was writing his books. So the question becomes, what brought it all on? Advanced syphilis has long been the most popular theory, but it's not one that's now accepted by doctors. Nietzsche showed none of the symptoms that you usually get with that disease, such as slurred speech, a blank face and slow reflexes. And while some sort of brain tumour is possible, it would have been a tumour that took a strangely long time to kill him. Recent research at Ghent University Hospital in Belgium suggests that the philosopher simply 'suffered from a psychiatric illness with depression' that slowly devolved into 'a profound dementia'.

One question, though. If you have a serious psychiatric illness, what's a good way to make it way worse? That's right: hallucinogenic drugs. Prone as he was to 'a laundry list of ailments', Hitler's favourite philosopher took drugs every day, and is seems fair to assume that they might have influenced his thought process. To deal with his various ailments including sensitivity to light, chronic constipation and bouts of dysentery, diarrhoea, and vomiting, he liked to self-medicate with chloral hydrate, a sedative that is not often used to sedate because it can make you hallucinate.

Also a fan of opium, together with potassium bromide, Nietzsche once described to his friend Resa von Schirnhofer how the drugs made him feel. 'When he closed his eyes, he saw an abundance of fantastic flowers, winding and intertwining, constantly growing and changing forms and colours in exotic luxuriance, sprouting one out of the other. "I never get any rest," he complained.'

It seems the 19th century's most influential philosopher was also its most wasted.

THE SECRET OF LIFE

Was biology's great breakthrough due to LSD?

> 'LSD is a catalyst and amplifier of mental process. If properly used it could become something like the microscope or telescope of psychiatry.'
>
> — Dr Stanislav Grof

Cambridge, England, 1953. Cobblestones, colleges, ivy, etc. Are you there? Can you picture the scene?

Well, now imagine two scruffy-looking men swaggering into a quaint little pub, the centuries-old Eagle on Free School Lane. One of them is 37 and dressed a bit like a bookmaker. The other's 25 and has god-awful hair. In loud, cocky voices, they order two pints of bitter even though it is barely midday. The pair tell a patron that they've decided to celebrate, for they have just that morning discovered 'the secret of life'.

Later that day the 37-year-old tells his wife the same thing. But just like my partner whenever I make such pronouncements, she doesn't believe him and is a little dismissive. 'You were always coming home and saying things like that,' Odile Crick told her husband in later years, 'so naturally I thought nothing of it.'

And just like my partner, she was wrong. These two 'bad boys of biology' may well have been 'arrogant', 'brash', 'annoying' and 'insufferable', as they were so often described, but that didn't mean that they were prone to exaggerate. On that cold February morning in 1953, they had indeed discovered something of more than passing importance: they had discovered the molecular structure of deoxyribonucleic acid, the substance that stores the genetic information of each and every living thing, and passes it on to their kids. The substance which proves that Man is indeed an ape, and that God is (if not untrue, then) unnecessary. The substance that then went on to revolutionise medicine, farming, forensics and crime shows, and may one day change computing as well. A substance that's better known as 'DNA'.

That all living things have DNA was already known in the 1950s, but (just like my in-depth knowledge of *Asterix* comics) it was knowledge that was of next to no use. Scientists didn't know exactly what this 'golden molecule' looked like, or how it carried genes from one living thing to the next. Francis Crick and James Watson won their Nobel prizes by working out how this 'code of life' all comes together, chemically speaking – the answer being that it's two long strands of phosphate nucleotides that sort of twist around each other like a long spiral staircase, bouncing genes back and forth.

Or something like that anyway. You may be gathering that I am not a scientist.

But back to drugs. One of the interesting things about Crick and Watson's earth-shattering discovery is that it was accomplished in just 18 short months, and it was accomplished with balls, sticks and glue. Rather than carry out original research or conduct molecular experiments of their own, the pair drew on findings in other fields (such as physics and X-ray crystallography) to make 3D models of what they felt DNA *ought* to look like, and then did little bits of chemistry to see if it did. It was an approach that relied on 'brilliant intuition' far more than painstaking research.

And here's a question for you, dear reader. Did that brilliant intuition in turn rely on LSD? The *Daily Mail* suggested as much in an article published ten days after Francis Crick's 2004 death (timing that, coincidentally or not, meant they couldn't get sued). 'Crick was high on LSD when he discovered the secret of life!' it read. According to that article, the now-dead scientist had told friends that back in the day he and his fellow boffins frequently used LSD to free up and sharpen their minds. Preconceptions are the enemy of imagination, or so the theory goes, and it's only by looking at the world from a different angle that we can see what has always been hidden.

This claim has spread all over the internet, but when we get down to brass tacks, is it actually true? This is the *Daily Mail*, after all: we're not talking about actual journalism. Are 'well-known psychedelic explorers' such as Graham Hancock right to insist that Crick's 'supreme achievement of scientific rationalism ... came to him in an altered, even mystical state of consciousness'.

Well, we'll probably never know. It's pretty clear that Crick enjoyed marijuana at the time (and considered bans on it to be both 'immoral' and 'unworkable'). But LSD would have been a hard thing to get your hands on in 1953, even for a well-connected chemist.

On the other hand, as he cheerfully pointed out in a 1998 interview, you 'only need 150 micrograms to have all these funny experiences ... It's minute.'

'And what experiences might one have?' the interviewer inquired.

'Well, typically, different ones act in different ways,' Crick replied. 'But a common thing is to see colours more vividly, for example, and often to see things move in a way when they're not actually moving, and things of that sort. So they boost up in some way the activities of what you might call the colour parts of the brain and the moving parts of the brain and so on.'

Not quite an admission, but certainly not a denial. I guess the bad boy's relationship with LSD is just another one of life's little secrets.

GREAT SCIENTIFIC TRIPS

Steve Jobs, 2011

'Taking LSD was a profound experience, one of the most important things in my life. LSD shows you that there's another side to the coin, and you can't remember it when it wears off, but you know it. It reinforced my sense of what was important – creating great things instead of making money, putting things back into the stream of history and of human consciousness as much as I could.'

The entrepreneur and inventor speaking to his biographer.

Professor Carl Sagan, 1969

'The illegality of cannabis is outrageous, an impediment to full utilization of a drug which helps produce the serenity and insight, sensitivity and fellowship so desperately needed in this increasingly mad and dangerous world.'

The groundbreaking astrophysicist in an essay written under pseudonym during his student days.

Professor Kary Mullis, 1994

'Back in the 1960s and early '70s I took plenty of LSD. A lot of people were doing that in Berkeley back then. And I found it to be a mind-opening experience. It was certainly much more important than any courses I ever took.'

The Nobel Prize-winning biochemist and LSD fan in an interview for California Monthly.

Dr John C Lilly, 1974

'In the province of the mind, what one believes to be true is true or becomes true, within certain limits to be found experientially and experimentally.'

The neuroscientist and LSD-fan in his book The Human Biocomputer.

Paul Erdös, 1971

'Before, when I looked at a piece of blank paper my mind was filled with ideas. Now all I see is a blank piece of paper.'

The renowned mathematician on the time he (briefly) quit amphetamines to prove to his friends he wasn't addicted.

HEART-STARTERS

Amphetamines & cocaine

Deepest, darkest Peru wasn't just the home of young Paddington Bear. It was also called home by the ancient Peruvians: people who ate, slept and shagged about 8000 years ago, and have since spent their time decomposing.

But these people didn't just eat, sleep and shag. They also liked to chew the plant that gives us cocaine. Traces of ancient chewed-up coca leaves have been found all over that country's Nanchoc Valley, in amongst little piles of burned-and-scraped rocks. (Burning a rock creates lime on the surface, which when scraped off and chewed in combination with coca leaves will release even more of those good-time chemicals.) It's a discovery that makes coke one of humanity's most time-honoured customs, like hunting, gathering and hating John Laws.

And the discoveries certainly don't end there. Thanks to assorted dental remains, ancient bits of mummy hair and various old pots, scientists can now confirm that coca was chewed in *most* ancient South American civilisations, including Nazca, Moche, Tiwanaku, Chiribaya and Inca. If aliens ever came to Earth in search of a good time, they wouldn't have bothered visiting any of the other continents: South America was where the party was at.

But while aliens never came (we think), the same can't be said about colonists. When Spanish and Portuguese soldiers turned up in South America in the late 1400s and started to shoot/rape/enslave everyone in sight, they didn't just send lots of silver back home – they also sent back a plant that was worth its weight in gold. 'Coca wine' became a major medicine in Europe, even amongst folks who weren't ill.

For many doctors this leaf was so much more than a leaf: it was nothing less than the 'elixir of life'. Some began to research its properties, in the hope that it might one day be 'used as a substitute for food'.

Eventually, that research met with success. In 1859, a German chemist called Albert Niemann finally managed to isolate the coca leaf's active ingredient, which he logically enough decided to label 'cocaine'. Within decades, the white stuff was being used as an anaesthetic in all sorts of surgeries and as a 'medicine' for all sorts of disease.

However, by 1900 it had become clear that the wonder drug had a few cons as well as pros – and that those cons included madness and death. Most governments started to make it illegal, a fact that some day might well affect sales.

Which brings us to another now largely illegal 'medicine', a heart-starter that found its feet in 1887. For it was then that – inspired by the elixir of life – a Romanian chemist called Lazăr Edeleanu turned his microscope to another exotic plant that was known to put pep in one's step. From *ma huang*, an ancient staple of Chinese medicine, he synthesised a brand new product, which he called 'amphetamine sulphate'. A product that people these days tend to call 'speed'.

Much like my cooking, most of my wardrobe and every single 'crap' word of my unpublished novel, Edeleanu's genius failed to be appreciated in his own lifetime, but in the 1930s, interest began to pick up. The first step came when a German company now known as GlaxoSmithKline used it to make a brand-new decongestant. Whether or not 'Benzedrine' actually cleared the nose, there was no doubt that it could really open your eyes – and give the rest of your body a buzz. Customers reported feeling 'a sense of well-being and a feeling of exhilaration' while on the stuff, together with 'lessened fatigue'.

If you think that sounds like a product that people would buy, your thinking is entirely correct. Germany quickly became a hive of amphetamine production – with the surprising result that its runners became way, way quicker. German Olympians did strangely well in the 1930s, presenting Herr Hitler with a heap of gold medals.

What happened after that? To find out, just turn the page.

Early evidence of coca use

- c. 6000 BCE – Evidence of chewed coca used by foraging societies found beneath a house in Peru
- c. 2500–1800 BCE – Coca leaves discovered in the Huaca Prieta settlement in Peru
- c. 2100 BCE – Ceramic containers found in Ecuador thought to have been used in coca chewing by the Valdivia culture
- c. 1000 BCE – Analysis of mummified human remains in Chile indicates the use of coca
- c. 100–800 BCE – Coca leaves and Moche pots illustrating a bulging cheek recovered from tombs in Peru

Nicknames for coke

- Blow
- Bolivian marching powder
- Charlie
- Nose candy
- Snow

Nicknames for amphetamines

- Meth
- Ice
- Speed
- Pills
- Uppers

Cocaine pros

- Feelings of euphoria
- Increased energy
- Grandiosity
- Clear-headedness
- Elevated mood

Cocaine cons

- Feelings of restlessness
- Irritability and anxiety
- Paranoia
- Muscle twitches or tics
- Increased heart rate

Cocaine big-time cons

- Chronic, extreme fatigue
- Unrelenting headaches
- Abdominal pain
- Heart arrhythmias and heart attack
- Significant weight loss
- Widespread ischemic vascular disease
- Strokes
- Seizures

Amphetamines pros

- Quicker reaction times
- Energy/wakefulness
- Excitement
- Attentiveness/concentration
- Feelings of euphoria

Amphetamines cons

- Dry mouth
- Nausea
- Headache
- Anxiety
- Hostility

Amphetamines big-time cons

- Paranoia
- Hallucinations
- Violent behaviour
- Respiratory problems
- Psychosis
- Dangerously high blood pressure
- Stroke
- Heart attack

SELF-MEDICATION

Doctors on drugs

'If all the medicine in the world were thrown into the sea, it would be bad for the fish and good for humanity.'

Professor OW Holmes

A doctor is supposed to set an example, to be clean-living, healthy and pure. No one wants a GP with brownish-yellow teeth. Or pinpricks in his arms. Or a deviated septum. No one wants a GP who likes to sample the pills they prescribe, or who offers to cut you a deal on 'some really choice meds'.

It may come as a blow, then, to discover that the chances of encountering this kind of doctor aren't so very low. It turns out that quite a few physicians are just a teensy bit drug-addled – many of the folks who we charge with keeping us healthy aren't necessarily doing such a great job when it comes to themselves.

Don't believe me? Well, neither would I. But how about the *Journal of Addiction Medicine*? In 2013 its researchers found that no less than 69 per cent of doctors have abused prescription medicine at some time or another in order 'to relieve stress and physical or emotional pain'. A separate study estimated that up to 15 per cent of physicians are prone to drug or alcohol abuse, compared to an average in the wider community of around 9 per cent. It appears that 'the most common method … is for the doctor to request a particular drug for a particular patient but then … use it for him or herself,' as an anaesthetist recently admitted to the Melbourne Magistrates Court.

He certainly wouldn't have had to tell Florence Nightingale. The founder of modern nursing (and owner of one of the all-time great surnames), Nightingale is famous for recruiting and training dozens of ordinary women to look after British soldiers during the Crimean War. Before 'the lady with the lamp' did her stuff, doctors didn't have professional, trained nurses to help them – which, needless to say, was bad news for us patients. Nightingale's nurses saved thousands of lives in the 1850s, and the systems and processes that they created have saved many millions since.

But Nightingale herself probably needed help too. After she came down with a minor fever during the war, she turned to opium to try and relieve it. And it was a 'cure' that she seems to have stuck with for the rest of her days, long after said fever was gone. A full-blown hypochondriac, she spent the final 20 years of her life stuck in a bed, complaining incessantly of insomnia, weakness and pain: nagging, vague and mysterious symptoms that could only be 'helped' by injections of opium.

Somewhat more productive during the time was one William Halstead, a 19th-century New Yorker now called 'the father of modern surgery'. The inventor of the radical mastectomy, the surgical glove and various still-used treatments for gallstones and hernias, as described by his fellow surgeon Lord Moynihan, Halstead was all about 'light, swift, sparing movements with the sharpest of knives' in an age where most surgeons essentially worked with an axe. It's because of Halstead's techniques that today's operations don't tend to kill us, or at least lead to gangrene.

But even geniuses can have their little flaws. Halstead's involved injecting cocaine into his limbs every single day of his life, and then following it up with some morphine every night. So terrible was his addiction to cocaine that the surgeon eventually became unable to operate without it, once leaving a patient screaming, writhing and bleeding on the table because he had to go home to get his next fix. It was not what you'd call first-class customer service, though God knows it's better than Telstra's.

Could it be, though, that coke was actually a *help* during Halstead's long, draining and stress-filled career? Could it have given him more energy and focus? Provided that sort of obsessive, relentless, clear-headed precision that maniacal overachievers all clearly need?

Sigmund Freud may well have had a thought or two on this subject, because it just so happens he was a cokehead himself. Just like Halstead, who first used the 'wonder drug' to see whether it could be an anaesthetic, Dr Freud's interest in the white stuff was purely medicinal, until there came a day when it wasn't.

The father of psychoanalysis first became interested in the drug in 1884, as a young physician making his way in Vienna. 'In my last serious depression, I took cocaine,' he wrote to a colleague, 'and a small dose lifted me to the heights in a wonderful fashion. I am just now collecting the literature for a song of praise to this magical substance.'

But within months he was doing more than acquiring literature. After starting to take 'very small doses of it regularly against depression and against indigestion and with the most brilliant of success', he had acquired what you might call a serious habit. Along with 'exhilaration and lasting euphoria, which in no way differs from the normal euphoria of the healthy person', Freud reported experiencing 'an increase in self-control' and far greater 'capacity for work'.

'In other words, you are simply more normal, and it is soon hard to believe that you are under the influence of a drug. If all goes well I will write an essay on it, and I expect it will win its place in therapeutics by the side of morphine ...'

Needless to say, all did not go well. We now know cocaine is a bit like *The Bachelor*, or a novel by Dan Brown. A little pinch every now and then is just a bit of fun, but enjoy it all the time and your brain soon becomes mush.

'I need a lot of cocaine,' Freud confessed to a colleague three years later, probably while shivering or dripping cold sweat. He managed to kick the habit not too long after that and was no doubt a happier man for it. But, as a *psychotherapist*, it's worth wondering whether he would ever have gone on to such heights if he'd not spend a few years going a tiny bit nuts.

The first rung on Freud's ladder to greatness, after all, was his iconic book *The Interpretation of Dreams*. More or less the bible of psychoanalysis, it introduced the idea that dreams are a tool for self-discovery, something that can help uncover what he called our 'subconscious'. (It also gave us the Oedipal complex, plus the idea that pretty much everything symbolises a penis.)

So what inspired this hefty tome? The answer is a dream that Freud himself had. And, as Howard Markel notes, it 'was indeed a dream about cocaine use'. Or, rather, it was a dream about the problems that resulted from operating on a patient while he – Freud – was on cocaine.

Say what?

Back to Markel: 'He dreamed that he was at a party, and [the patient] came to him ... there were syringes and cocaine and scabs all around. And she accused him in front of this gathering, [saying] "you nearly killed me, this was terrible".'

When Freud woke up the next day, he 'wondered about this and said, well, I had this dream because I'm such a concerned physician that if any of my patients have a bumpy course, I feel it as well'. But in reality 'Freud had this dream because he was rather upset and nervous that he nearly killed her while treating her [while] under the influence', and in time he realised this.

It was an instructive example of the revelatory power of dreams, the fundamental idea that defined Freud's career. Underneath the theory of the subconscious lies a thick white seam of cocaine.

THE POWER NAPPER

Famous inventions that come back to cocaine

'Coke is pure kick. It lifts you straight up, a mechanical lift that starts leaving you as soon as you feel it.'

William S Burroughs

'Success,' said Thomas Edison, 'is the product of the severest kind of mental and physical application.' As catchy sayings go, I think we can all agree that this was not his best work. Edison, after all, was the man who gave us 'Genius is 1 per cent inspiration, 99 per cent perspiration', a saying that's straight out of the very top shelf.

But I think we can all agree that both aphorisms express the same basic idea – and so indeed did the inventor's whole life. Thomas Edison was one of those up-at-dawn, slave-all-night workaholic types who see their friends and family about three times a year. You don't patent 2332 different inventions by having a full and rounded life, after all; you do it by hustling and bustling, and sweating and fretting, and working day after day at your desk.

'He regarded sleep as a waste of time ... a heritage from our cave days,' says James Maas of the man whose 100-hour work weeks gave us electric lights, recorded music and the movie camera. Essentially the father of the light bulb – and a sort of uncle of batteries and the telephone – Edison rarely slept for more than a few hours a night, and frequently went days without sleeping at all.

'Most people oversleep,' he wrote in 1921, and that 'makes them unhealthy and inefficient. The person who sleeps eight or ten hours a night is never fully asleep and never fully awake – they have only different degrees of doze through the 24 hours ... For myself, I never found need of more than four or five hours' sleep in the 24. I never dream. It's real sleep. When by chance I have taken more I wake dull and indolent. We are always hearing people talk about "loss of sleep" as a calamity (but the real calamity is the) loss of time, vitality and opportunities (that comes from oversleeping instead). Just to satisfy my curiosity I have gone through files of the *British Medical Journal* and could not find a single case reported of anybody being hurt by loss of sleep.'

In fact, when you got down to it, the man who's been called 'the greatest inventor that ever lived' could really see 'no reason why men should go to bed at all'.

So when it came to the men who worked in his private ~~sweatshop~~ laboratory, Edison did his best to make that they didn't. Every single researcher was 'expected to keep pace with him', wrote John Hubert

Greusel of this fabled workers' paradise. 'When they fell from sheer exhaustion, he seemed to begrudge the brief hours they were sleeping.'

'At first the boys had some difficulty in keeping awake,' reported Mr Dream Boss himself of his WorkChoices-like system, a Liberal Party wet dream, which, like all systems, had a few early kinks. 'They would go to sleep under stairways and in corners, so we employed watchers to bring them out, and in time they got used to it.'

It all sounds extremely unpleasant. But that's not all, for it was also unjust. While 99 per cent of Edison's genius may well have come from perspiration, a big part of that perspiration came down to a product that he kept to himself.

A product that was, of course, cocaine.

The 'Wizard of Menlo Park' was a daily drinker of Vin Mariani, Vin Mariani being a then-popular brand of 'nerve tonic' that was essentially just cocaine and wine. Containing 7.2 milligrams of coca leaves for every fluid ounce of Bordeaux, it was a sure-fire way to put pep in your step – or, as the makers put it, 'restore health, strength and energy'.

Edison's success definitely came down to ~~exploitation~~ hard work. But how much of that hard work was due to hard drugs? On balance, I'd say that genius is probably about 1 per cent inspiration, 68 per cent perspiration and 34 per cent pure grade cocaine.

A WONDER OF SCIENCE

While 'genius' may not be quite the right word to describe Ozzy Osborne, 'scientific miracle' could well hit the spot. In 2007, scientists sequenced Osborne's genome in order to better understand how, exactly, he's still alive after all those years of hard drugs and booze. The results revealed that Osborne has an increased predisposition for alcohol dependence (around six times higher than average). Researchers also discovered a mutation on the regulatory region of his ADH4 gene, a gene associated with alcoholism. The next X-Men movie could be writing itself.

A HAZARDOUS JOURNEY

How the crew of the Endurance
somehow managed to endure

'Cocaine is like really evil coffee.'

Courtney Love

The modern world has its fair share of problems: melting icecaps, rising depression, the continued existence of Andrew Bolt. But it's fair to say that things were once worse. The olden days were all dirt, disease and second-rate dentistry. For every golden-haired damsel in distress or chivalrous knight in bright, shiny armour, you had about a million peasants who spent their days in a field wearing lice and a mouldy old sack.

But the olden days did have at least one good quality: there were always more things to explore. Captain Cook may not have had Netflix, but he could travel to an unknown land. Christopher Columbus never got a chance to use an emoji, but he did get to 'discover' a continent. 'The Age of Exploration' may have been bad news for pretty much everyone outside of Europe, but if you were an explorer, it must have been pretty fun.

But by 1900 said Age was over. Apart from a fair bit of ocean floor and one or two Himalayan peaks, the South Pole was the only place on the planet that European explorers had not yet conquered and mapped. Many had tried and many had died – I'm told that this vast, frozen wasteland can at times get a bit chilly.

In December 1913 the following ad appeared in an English newspaper: 'Men wanted for hazardous journey,' it read. 'Small wages, bitter cold, long months of complete darkness. Safe return doubtful. Honour and recognition in case of success.'

To my mind, this doesn't sound especially appealing, but it takes all sorts to explore a world. Ernest Shackleton received around 5000 responses to his public appeal to board his ship, *The Endurance*. Eventually 28 lucky men were chosen to venture into the 'the heart of the great white alone'.

And it wasn't long before they were all regretting it. About 1500 kilometres south of their last glimpse of civilisation – if 'civilisation' is the right word for a whaling station – the 300-tonne *Endurance* suddenly found itself trapped amid falling pack ice. Somehow afloat, but without the ability to sail, it drifted helplessly in a frozen prison for months before running aground.

I myself would consider this a good moment to panic – or at least collapse to the floor for a nice, quiet sob. Shackleton, however, was made of much sterner stuff. Facing below-freezing temperatures and a shortage of food, swirling blizzards and the onset of scurvy, he had to choose between staying put (and thus dying slowly), or rowing out in a tiny wooden boat to try and find help (and thus probably dying quite fast).

Rather heroically, he chose the latter. On 24 April 1916 the explorer set out with five men, a few oars, not much food and no roof to try and find a little whaling station somewhere in the north. As a one biographer put it, it was like an insect trying to swim in a tidal wave. It was almost as bad as the Boxing Day sales.

But what's amazing is that they actually made it. After being left to their frostbitten fate, the 22 remaining members of Shackleton's expedition were shocked to see a rescue ship appear on the horizon on 30 August. The Shack was back, and more dashing than ever. Later named Sir Ernest, he was a real-life knight in shining parka.

'If you're a leader, a fellow that other fellows look to, you've got to keep going,' was how the man himself later summarised those 'many months of want and hunger' in the 'seething chaos of tortured water'. 'Difficulties are just things to overcome, after all.'

And really, who am I to quibble? The last *Boys Own*-type difficulty that I had to overcome involved removing a spider from my daughter's bedroom. And I overcame it by calling my daughter.

But if I *was* to quibble, I might say this: heroic, death-defying journeys are probably a little easier to accomplish when you're off-chops on pure-grade cocaine. When Shackleton and his men set off for the South Pole, they brought enough 'medical supplies' for a rave. Included in these supplies were opium (for diarrhoea) and a cannabis/chilli pepper cocktail that was designed to cure colic. The ship also contained gallons of whiskey (for warmth, of course), together with cocaine eye drops (a supposed cure for snow blindness).

But what must have really saved the day out there in the ice, wind and waves, was a brand of cocaine tablets sold under them the name of 'Forced March'. The Red Bull of its day, Forced March didn't promise to 'give you wings', but I'm pretty sure it would have helped you to row.

TANK CHOCOLATE

Could the Nazis have conquered Europe without crystal meth?

'The men began spontaneously reporting that they felt better. They began marching in orderly fashion again, their spirits improved, and they became more alert.'

A German doctor in 1942, after giving Pervitin to 'exhausted' troops.

In most jobs, you're 'unfit for work' if you take drugs. If you're an American fighter pilot, you can be unfit if you don't.

I do not lie. (Well, not about this, anyway. It's possible that my last tax return had one or two grey areas, and that I've never actually read all of *Ulysses*.) It turns out that the US Air Force dispenses 'go pills' intended to keep its pilots alert and awake when they fly off on long missions. In real life, Maverick, Ice Man, Goose and the gang wouldn't have just spent their time on the ground playing topless volleyball. They would have also been busy signing forms with headings such as 'Informed Consent for Use of Dextroamphetamine as a "Go Pill" in Military Operations'. If you want to be a top gun, you must be prepared to get high.

'We know that fatigue in aviation kills,' says Colonel Peter Demitry, chief of the US Air Force surgeon-general's science and technology division. 'This is a life-and-death insurance policy that saves lives. [Amphetamines are] the gold standard for anti-fatigue.'

And they've been the gold standard for quite a while. Amphetamines powered bombing missions in Iraq in 1991, in Kosovo in 1999 and throughout every stage of the Afghan campaign. And in Vietnam, 'pep pills' were handed out like candies whenever soldiers set off on jungle missions or ambushes that required lengthy waits.

In 1971, a House Select Committee found that the army distributed no less than 225 million 'dexys' in Nam – and that was just in the late 1960s. 'We had the best amphetamines available and they were supplied by the US Government' a veteran recently told *The Atlantic* (presumably while wearing fluro pants and a visor, and on his way to the nearest club). The article also featured an interview with a navy commando who reported that the little orange pills 'gave you a sense of bravado, as well as keeping you awake'. 'Every sight and sound was heightened. You were wired into it all, and at times you felt really invulnerable.'

Or as another veteran put rather less elegantly elsewhere, 'Take 100 non-aggressive men and give them all enough speed and you end up with the equivalent of 150 men that'll kill anything that moves. And if they have to, they'll kill it with their bare hands.'

Speed kills, so to speak.

But while, as the philosopher Nick Land put it, Vietnam may have represented 'a decisive point of intersection between pharmacology and the technology of violence', it certainly wasn't the first pharmacological war. That honour goes to World War II. As Brook Durham writes, 'Technological advances in the 1930s and 1940s created new possibilities for conducting operations across great distances, at any time of the day, including night warfare. Mechanised vehicles in the army, navy and air force could operate indefinitely, so long as there was fuel. Advancements in radio communications and radar imaging allowed combat operations to continue throughout the night. The "blitzkrieg" style of warfare required near-superhuman efforts to equip rapidly advancing armies with munitions and supplies. The weakest link in this unrelenting style of warfare was the soldier, who found less time than ever for sleep and rejuvenation.'

But why worry about a weak link when you have a strong pill? Throughout World War II, Britain and the US are said to have given their soldiers over *150 million* crude amphetamine tablets by the name of Benzedrine sulphate. Dexedrine and methedrine also helped Allied soldiers to stay awake while they drove tanks, sailed ships, flew planes, kept watch and spent weeks in U-class submarines.

Japan's kamikaze pilots also got in on the act. They're said to have washed amphetamines down with buckets of sake before every suicide mission.

But it was the Nazis who clearly led the way when it came to making the most of their 'medicine'. Hitler & co are thought to have handed out about 200 million pills of 'Pervitin' to his blond-haired bringers of death – Pervitin being a handy product that, these days, we call 'crystal meth'.

Nicknamed 'tank chocolate' and 'pilot's salt', Pervitin more or less started out as an experiment-on-the-side during the Nazi's 1939 invasion of Poland. But it was an experiment that proved so extraordinarily successful that they made manufacturing more a first-level priority. The following year's conquest of France (a campaign that in less than six weeks accomplished what Germany's World War I soldiers couldn't do in four years) changed warfare forever with its rapid-fire, day-and-night movements of soldiers. Blitzkrieg was a brand new form of 'lightning war' that rendered old technology such as trenches and forts obsolete.

But would it have even been possible if the Nazi soldiers had not been so blitzed?

GREAT AUSTRALIAN HYPE-UPS

Malcolm Fraser, 1986

'They were having him on. Poor old boy. Someone must have slipped him a mickey finn as soon as he walked in. He rang me up and told me about it when he got back to his own hotel.

'He might have gone off with someone here or there at some time but he wouldn't go to a bar to meet someone on the off chance – they were setting him up. Poor old boy. It's really horrible. He was so embarrassed. And still is.'

Tamie Fraser, on the night her husband wound up in the lobby of a dodgy Memphis hotel, with no memory and wearing nothing but a (small) towel.

Wayne Carey, 2008

'We realise when we do drugs we're as silly as one another. If we are to go forward together, we have to make those important changes. I really think I had to hit rock bottom, which I have now, before I was forced to make these changes.'

The former AFL star after admitting to a cocaine problem in the wake of violent 'clashes' with his girlfriend Kate Neilson.

Wayne Carey, 2012

'It was only a matter of time before you were caught again! #douchebag.'

Kate Neilson, tweeting after reports emerge that traces of cocaine had been detected on Carey during a visit to inmates of Barwon Heads prison.

The NRL, 2017

'These guys were my heroes, I looked up to them and wanted them to like me. I had something they wanted and I wanted them to like me.'

The apparently rather lonely Adrian Mark Crowther on selling cocaine to two NRL stars.

DER JUNKIE

How drugs helped Hitler and Churchill

> *'I'm not addicted to cocaine. I just like the way it smells.'*
>
> Richard Pryor

Don't get me wrong, I'm happy to give it a go – but I'm pretty sure that constant, daily, low-level drunkenness wouldn't really bring out my intellectual best. If I was to start every day with champagne and a whiskey, then get stuck into a couple of claret-and-sodas as the morning progressed, I'd suspect I'd be wanting some coffee over lunch, rather than a waiter to break out the cognac. And if my afternoon was then filled with still more champagne, one or two more claret-and-sodas and a pre-dinner sherry, I can promise you that I'd spend dinner snoring my head off rather than making cocktails and asking for port.

But that's just one of many reasons why I'm not Winston Churchill, a man who not only managed to walk straight while drinking like this, day in and day out, but also managed to win World War II. The Great

Man worked 18-hour days during the war while having blood alcohol levels that would wipe out a wildebeest. Yet he seemed to feel, if not Great, then at least perfectly fine, despite also being overweight and in his late-60s.

Where on earth did all that energy come from?

The answer seems to be speed. Churchill's private physician Lord Moran prescribed him a 'very heavy duty' range of drugs to relieve the symptoms of heavy boozing: hangovers, fatigue, sleeplessness, jitters and depression. England's greatest ever prime minister popped pills like they were candy.

But in this (and every single other way), it seems fair to say that Hitler was worse. Churchill's opponent throughout World War II was more than his match when it came to abusing hard drugs. Thanks to his even more private physician, the Führer is thought to have downed around 80 drugs a day during the final three years of his life.

Sometimes described as a 'phony' – and at other times as a 'quack' or a 'charlatan' – Dr Theodore Morell became known as 'the Reichsmaster of injections' in the late 1930s, when the genocidal one was suffering from stomach pains. A 'vitamin' shot containing crystal meth soon put things right, and before long Hitler was having several such shots a day, along with tranquilisers to help bring him back down in the evenings.

And that was just the beginning. When the Führer developed sinus problems in 1941, cocaine eye drops were found to help, just as morphine shots helped control his eczema. With bull's semen, baritone and belladonna also on the daily regimen, along with dihydroxy codeine and crystal meth, Allied doctors later concluded that Dr Morell's medication was slowly poisoning Hitler and was actually responsible for many of his aliments.

When the Allies entered Europe on D-Day and started bombing their way towards Berlin, they took out the factories that made the Nazi pep pills, Eukodal and Pervitin – and were Hitler's last remaining sources of crystal meth. Footage of him weeks later (and just days before his suicide) reveal a sweaty, pale and pathetic-looking specimen 'stabbing at his skin with a pair of golden tweezers'.

'Everyone describes the bad health of Hitler in those final days,' says the German historian Norman Ohler of this 'bowed and drooling' shadow of a man. 'It has been suggested that he was suffering from Parkinson's disease [but to me] it's pretty clear that it was partly withdrawal.'

'It must have been pretty awful,' he adds with a grin. 'He's losing a world war, and he's coming off drugs.'

The important question, though, is why Hitler lost that world war in the first place – and whether all that drug abuse was in any small way to blame. We need to remember that, after comfortably conquering most of Europe, he decided to declare war on both the US and Russia – two decisions that were nothing short of suidical, given those countries' much bigger size. He took both decisions against the advice of his generals, and he probably took them while high on cocaine. On a drug that can make a man feel invincible.

Either way, while Dr Morell continued to give him 'drugs that made him feel invulnerable and on top of the situation', the actual situation went from bad to much worse. Writes Ohler: 'The generals kept telling him, "We need to change our tactics. We need to end this. We are going to lose the war," and he didn't want to hear it ... He used this strong drug that made him euphoric even when reality wasn't looking euphoric at all.'

According to another historian, with the somewhat unlikely name of Chauncey Mabe, Hitler's many military misjudgements show a man whose 'delusions divorced him completely from reality'. He simply 'overstretched German troops', moving many into 'suicidal positions'. He even 'planned a defence of Berlin using non-existent battalions.'

When it was all over, Professor Nassir Ghaemi says, 'some of [Dr Morell's] American interrogators wondered whether he was a double agent, trying to make Hitler so dysfunctional that he just couldn't win'.

'AN ANXIOUS, CONFUSED INSOMNIAC'

How amphetamines sped up the end of the Empire

'Dominique offered me a bennie – Benzedrine? – to elevate my spirits. Adamantly I told her, No thanks! I wanted to face what's called reality with my eyes open. I've made that a principle for my life. Sometimes I wonder if this has been a wise decision.'

Joyce Carol Oates

The Commonwealth Games weren't always about athletes from rich countries collecting a bagful of medals and giving the bronze ones to their family and friends. It wasn't always about crushing tiny island nations, which have two running tracks and an inflatable pool.

Actually, no, I take it all back. It's probably been like that from the start. But something that *has* changed is the name.

Yes, the name. It wasn't all that long ago that the Commonwealth Games were called the Empire Games, because said empire was actually a thing. Australians all sang 'Rule, Britannia!' because Britannia really did rule the waves. From the Caribbean in the west to Hong Kong in the east, Oxbridge graduates in bowler hats were very much still all big wigs.

But by the early 1950s, of course, those wigs were fraying: the Empire over which the sun never set was starting to fade into darkness. World War I had torn the heart out of the British economy, and World War II had removed both its kidneys. Ghana and Nigeria were both about to achieve independence, and India had already won it. Australia more or less saw itself as a standalone country, and so too did New Zealand and Canada. Even the Kenyans were starting to rise up and revolt, and there were rumblings in Cyprus and Malaya.

But the British Empire Games were still the 'British Empire Games', and ordinary Britons still expected to win it. 'People just weren't prepared to accept the nation's decline,' says historian Adrian Bingham. 'There was still this feeling that we were a great power [even though in reality] ... there were only two superpowers – the United States and the Soviet Union.'

So when did that delusion come to an end? When did Britons realise that while a quarter of the map was still pink, the real world was now red, white and blue? That the Lion and the Unicorn were both dead and buried, and that from now on they would be America's poodle?

The answer is 'during the Suez Crisis'. It was in July of 1956 that grim reality finally dawned. Britain's 'last fling of the Imperial dice', the crisis kicked off when one of those ungrateful former colonies decided to act like an independent country. Two years after the last British soldier left Egypt in 1954, that country's new president decided to nationalise the Suez Canal, an enormously valuable shipping route to oilfields of the East, which English and French investors still felt they owned.

The solution, in Queen Victoria's day, would have just been to declare war: get the swishy stick out of the cupboard and give those golliwogs a damn good thrashing. But given all the complex geopolitical realities of the new Cold War – chiefly the West's need to keep the Arab world on-side – it was clear that old-fashioned white imperialism was simply no longer an option.

Or rather, it was clear to everyone except Britain's PM. As Churchill's foreign secretary throughout World War II, Prime Minister Anthony Eden had already spent 'a lifetime at the cutting edge of British statesmanship'. He was far from a dopey George W Bush-type, who shouldn't even have been allowed to use scissors. But the Suez Crisis inexplicably saw him become just such a type: out of the blue, and behind closed doors, Eden arranged for Israel to launch an invasion of Egypt. The idea was that England would then have an excuse to invade as well in order to 'protect' the commercially important canal from the fighting.

And, in the event, that's exactly what happened – until the Americans found out and ordered the English to leave. 'Our closest ally pulled the plug,' says Corelli Barnett, author of *The Collapse of British Power*. 'We were told by them to go no further and to evacuate promptly. So we did. It was a complete fiasco.'

For Professor Simon Hall, the crisis was more than simply 'humiliating'. Insofar as it was 'played out before the eyes of the world,' it actually accelerated the break-up of the Empire. 'It was important internationally because it didn't so much destroy Britain's status as a global power but exposed its decline, which up until that point had been kept well hidden. [This] boosted the growing anti-colonial movement. Much of our empire was gone within ten years ... [It all] happened much quicker than people previously thought it would.'

So what the hell was Eden thinking? As Professor David Dutton puts it, 'it is difficult to understand' why this hitherto sober-minded, cautious and extremely canny statesman 'believed that he would get away with the Franco/Israeli plan and conceal it from the United States, unless you believe that his judgement was not what it was at its peak.'

So a better question might be: what was he *taking*?

This 'last attempt by a British government to do the old imperial thing' was engineered by a man who 'was seriously ill'. 'Weak and tired and desperately in need of a rest and probably on the verge of a nervous breakdown,' England's prime minister was recovering from a badly botched operation on his gall bladder that had left him exhausted and in constant pain.

And, as it happened, completely addicted to speed.

'It was not thought that I would lead an active life again. However, with the aid of (mild) drugs and stimulants, I have been able to do so,' Eden wrote in his diary. But 'since Nasser seized the Canal in July, I have been obliged to increase the drugs considerably and also increase the stimulants necessary to counteract the drugs.' Throughout the crisis, he later admitted, he was 'practically living on Benzedrine'.

The result was what one historian called 'an anxious, confused insomniac whose erratic behaviour became the talk of the corridors of power'. 'I find it difficult to accept the judgement that Anthony's health did not have a decisive influence at least on the conduct of his policy,' Eden's Parliamentary Private Secretary later wrote.

Without a drug that's now known to cause insomnia, overconfidence, anger and mood swings, 'I find it very hard to believe that he would have made such obvious miscalculations … He overestimated the importance of Nasser, Egypt, the Canal, even of the Middle East itself.' Anthony Eden would not have made all of those mistakes is he was healthy.

'Very jumpy, very nervy and very wrought', Eden resigned within weeks of the English retreat on, yes, the grounds of ill health.

The British Empire remains in ill-heath to this day.

YOUTHFUL VITALITY

How JFK's drug problems forever changed politics

> 'No president with his finger on the red button has any business taking stuff like that.'
> Dr Hans Kraus, JFK's orthopaedic surgeon

As the likes of Kim Beazley, Joe Hockey and Clive Palmer all know, it just doesn't pay to be a fat politician. It's all about being telegenic these days. The voters want vigour, fitness and dynamism – they want someone with bright eyes and white teeth. Jogging is how you get to the corridors of power ... jogging and a great deal of make-up. Plus nice hair, good clothes and a shave.

All this is a fairly modern development, if you go by some of the fat beardies who used to dwell in the Lodge. Australia's fourth PM, Sir George Reid, for example, looked like the kind of man who could have eaten the first three and still plenty of room for dessert.

Like most bad things, our obsession with looks can probably be traced back to America. Or more specifically to the America that came into being on 26 September 1960. 'It's one of those unusual points on the timeline of history where you can say things changed very dramatically,' says Professor Alan Schroeder. 'In this case, in a single night.'

What happened on that night was that the two candidates in that year's presidential election held the first ever televised debate. An extraordinary *74 million* Americans tuned in to see the 43-year-old John F Kennedy – a fresh-faced Democrat who 'looked to be radiating health' – take on the beady-eyed spiv, Richard Nixon. Pale, underweight and not long out of hospital, Tricky Dicky wasn't a looker at the best of times, and with that five o'clock shadow and ill-fitting grey suit, on this particular night he was looking his worst. He sweated and twitched and scowled and glared. He failed to apologise for having such a big nose.

That said, he seemed to debate pretty well. Polls of the thousands who listened in on the radio overwhelmingly judged Nixon the winner.

The millions of TV watchers, however, heard a different debate. Or rather, they all *saw* one. And what they saw was a shifty-looking big-nose face off against a handsome young man with great hair and some nice, even teeth. By a truly ridiculous margin, they judged hunk-of-spunk to have been the debate's winner.

And when the election rolled around, he duly won that as well. 'You couldn't wipe away the image people had seared in their brains from the first debate,' says Schroder. 'It was the TV more than anything else that turned the tide.'

'Before the television debates, most Americans didn't even see the candidates – they read about them, they saw photos of them,' explains the political analyst Larry Sabato. 'This allowed the public to judge candidates on a completely different basis. [Now] when parties are considering their candidates they ask: Who would look better on TV? Who comes across better?'

But for all that a picture is worth a thousand words, it's worth noting that in JFK's case, those words were all lies. Far from radiating health and vitality, that tanned sexpot had a long list of ailments. Severe asthma was one; severe allergies another. Then you had colitis, prostatitis, osteoporosis and a smattering of STDs. But even though he was also prone to stomach problems … and recurrent infections and fevers … and various brands of crippling back pain, JFK's most serious issue was actually Addison's disease. A once-fatal failure of the adrenal glands, it causes weakness, fatigue, joint pain, muscle pain, light-headedness, nausea and vomiting. And that's just on a good day.

So what gives? How was Kennedy able to bounce onto the debate stage full of zip, verve and charisma and change politics as a result?

The answer is our old friend, drugs. As historian Robert Dallek writes, the president's daily pharmacopoeia included 'steroids for his Addison's disease, painkillers for his back, antispasmodics for his colitis, antibiotics for urinary-tract infections, antihistamines for allergies and, on at least one occasion, an antipsychotic.' 'If a mosquito bites my brother,' Bobby Kennedy once quipped, 'then the mosquito dies.'

But while all that explains how JFK was able to stand up, is it enough to explain all the *verve*?

No. For that, we have to thank 'Dr Feelgood'. Eventually disbarred by the medical board and charged with 48 counts of unprofessional conduct, Dr Max Jacobson was notorious for his 'vitamin shots' – injections that mixed a few steroids and hormones with a whole heap of strengthening speed. Celebrity clients such as Truman Capote reported that they caused 'instant euphoria'. 'You feel like Superman,' he enthused. 'You're flying. Ideas come at the speed of light. You go 72 hours straight without so much as a coffee break. If it's sex you're after, you can go all night.'

In early 1960, 'Miracle Max' became JFK's doctor too – and the patient seemed to enjoy his fine work. Dr Feelgood became a regular visitor to the White House and occasional passenger on Airforce One, reportedly shooting JFK up three times before a big Russian summit.

Did he actually shoot him up before the debate too? That's what rumour says, and he was certainly present backstage.

Either way, it's worth remembering that when Russia tried to place nuclear missiles in Cuba a couple of years later, the Joint Chiefs of Staff all urged Kennedy to launch a 'pre-emptive strike'. While Kennedy decided to stick with diplomacy, and eventually managed to solve things peacefully, we can be pretty sure that the far, far more gung-ho Nixon would have been bombs-away had he been in the White House.

'Had [the president] done as the Joint Chiefs urged, it would have started a nuclear war from which nobody would have survived,' says

Kennedy's speechwriter Ted Sorensen. 'I think we should certainly be grateful that John F Kennedy won that debate.'

Had JFK not been on speed, the whole world might have come to a stop.

SPEEDING UP THE CREATIVE PROCESS

How great books sometimes rely on great drugs

> 'Let's say you're in a situation where crystal meth can help you. Like, I don't know, you have too many teeth.'
>
> — Dave Attell

Being a writer, believe it or not, can actually be a rather hard slog. Okay, it's not like going down a coal mine. But that's only because going down a coal mine is actually pretty well-paid. To put bread on the table, add cheese and dips and wash it all down with a full-bodied wine, a writer needs to pump out a few thousand words, not just once, but just about every day. They need to find all the right nouns, add all the right adjectives, and throw in some prepositions and verbs. It can all get a bit exhausting after a while, particularly if you're not entirely clear what a preposition is.

So is it really so very surprising that many writers get addicted to coffee? Voltaire supposedly drank up to 40 cups a day, while Balzac claimed to drink over 50. 'Coffee glides into one's stomach and sets all of one's mental processes in motion,' that Frenchman wrote of the drink that helped him to write for 18 hours a day – and also gave him 'horrible sweats [and] feebleness of the nerves'. The author of 90 novels (plus a few libraries' worth of essays, letters, plays and poems) died of a heart attack at age 51, and the only surprise was that he didn't die sooner.

Maybe a healthier approach would have been to take lots of cocaine? It certainly seemed to work for Robert Louis Stevenson. A lifelong invalid thanks to tuberculosis, and a long list of other lung problems, the Scottish author of *Treasure Island* treasured the sweet relief that the white stuff could bring. Legend has it that one night in 1885 he needed a lot more than usual, due to some particularly violent coughing that had brought on a haemorrhage. After few hours of fitful and nightmare-filled sleep – tossing, turning, yelping, sweating – he was woken up by his concerned wife. No need to worry, he cheerfully told her, he had just been 'dreaming a fine bogey tale'.

Also a profitable one. That nightmare formed the basis of *The Strange Case of Dr Jekyll and Mr Hyde*, Stephenson's classic novella about an ordinary, everyday, pleasant-enough man who is turned into a dark, savage beast by strange drugs. Still coked up to the gills and coughing like a madman, Stevenson wrote the 30,000-word first draft in under three days.

Graham Greene was equally productive a few decades later, when financial need suddenly required him to write two novels in the space of six weeks. Having heard from the likes of WH Auden that speed could work as a 'labour-saving device', that author decided to start having Benzedrine for breakfast and another tablet or two over lunch. But while the pills ended up giving us *The Confidential Agent*, and probably his best novel, *The Power and the Glory*, they didn't do much for Greene's personal life, or indeed the general state of his health.

'I was forcing the pace and I suffered for it,' he later wrote. 'Six weeks of a Benzedrine breakfast diet left my nerves in shreds and my wife suffered the result. At five o'clock I would return home with a shaking hand, a depression which fell with the regularity of a tropical rain, ready to find offense in anything, and to give offense for no cause. For long after the six weeks were over, I had to continue with smaller and smaller doses to break the habit.'

'The career of writing has its own curious forms of hell. Sometimes, looking back, I think that those Benzedrine weeks were more responsible than the separation of war and my own infidelities for breaking our marriage.'

Sartre, however, was much more sanguine when it came to his time with his little white chums. Here's a random passage from *The Critique of Dialectical Reason*, the philosophical work that first made his name. 'It should be noted that this regulatory totalisation realises my immanence in the group in the quasi-transcendence of the totalising third party; for the latter, as the creator of objectives or organiser of means, stands in a tense and contradictory relation of transcendence-immanence, so that my integration, though real in the here and now which define me, remains somewhere incomplete, in the here and now which characterise the regulatory third party. We see here the re-emergence of an element of alterity proper to the statute of the group, but which here is still formal: the third party is certainly the same, the praxis is certainly common everywhere; but a shifting dislocation makes it totalising when I am the totalised means of the group, and conversely.'

Got all that? If not, it may not altogether surprise you to learn that Sartre wrote all this shit on speed. The *Critique* was composed in a couple of months (which is about as long as you'll need to read its first chapter). The philosopher swallowed 20 pills a day to help him pump the thing out, followed by barbiturates every night so he could snatch some sleep.

He could have just read *On the Road*, Jack Kerouac's desperately boring Beat novel about a bunch of dudes who drive around America while drunk and on drugs. 'All first person, fast, mad, confessional [and] detailed,' he famously wrote the thing in just 21 days – a hair-raising speed that was, of course, due to speed, and which becomes rather less surprising when you read the result.

'Benny [Benzedrine] has made me see a lot,' Kerouac wrote to his Beat colleague Allen Ginsberg, neglecting to mention that it also made his legs swell up and lost him most of his hair. 'The process of intensifying awareness naturally leads to an overflow of old notions, and voila, new material wells up.'

It may not surprise you to learn that Kerouac died very early – and did not leave a good-looking corpse. In this, he was not unlike his fellow junkie, the unfortunately named Philip K Dick. *Blade Runner*,

Total Recall, *Minority Report* and more all owe their plots to the work of this pioneering sci-fi writer who 'popped as many as a thousand amphetamine pills a week'. Essentially uninterested in aliens and such like, Dick's books revolve around questions of reality and whether it's ... well ... *real*. As a man who felt sure that the CIA was brainwashing him, was temporarily 'possessed by the spirit of the prophet Elijah', and who 'often raved about seeing a giant metallic face floating above him in the sky', you'd suspect that these were questions that Dick asked himself quite a lot.

And questions that might not have arisen had he not been on drugs.

SURPRISING SONGS ABOUT COCAINE AND AMPHETAMINES

Art and drugs may go hand in hand, but that's not always clear to our ears. Here are some songs that you may not have realised are in fact all about drugs.

- *Life in the Fast Lane* (The Eagles)
- *Snowblind* (Black Sabbath)
- *Casey Jones* (The Grateful Dead)
- *Benny and the Jets* (Elton John)
- *Semi-Charmed Life* (Third Eye Blind)

COCA COLA CAPITALISM

Why the modern economy owes much to cocaine

> 'I remember thinking cocaine was subtle until I noticed I'd been awake for three weeks and didn't know any of the naked people passed out around me.'
>
> PJ O'Rourke

Have you ever googled 'Coca Cola capitalism'? Unless you're one of those odd people who enjoy macroeconomic theory, my suggestion would be that you just stick to porn. The basic idea, according to obscure academics who seem to love even-more-obscure words, is that the world's best-known soft drink essentially created the way today's corporations do business – and in so doing has screwed up the planet.

What they're talking about, essentially, is *outsourcing*. The Coca Cola Company does it a lot. It owns a recipe for syrup, the means to make it and ... well ... that's about it. Thousands of local franchisees all over the world pay for the privilege of doing everything else. Some grow the syrup's ingredients, some add the water, some make the bottles and some fill them up. Other franchisees pack said bottles onto trucks and still others transport them to shops. Ironically, considering the way it has made many people fat, Coke is the very definition of a lean operation.

'Coca Cola capitalism,' then, involves earning billions of dollars without any of the bother of owning factories or farms. It involves encouraging – or at least facilitating – exploitation by subcontractors and handballing on any and all risks and costs. Corporations such as Coke are essentially a sort of stockbroker: an economic parasite that creates next to nothing other than money from the global flow of its 'brand'.

Okay, rant over.

The question we're left with is, how did this happen? How did a little sugar-water company from Hicksville, Georgia somehow clock onto the secret of capitalism, and in so doing, become a global behemoth? Good luck? Good management? Bad morals?

The short answer seems to be happenstance: Coca Cola capitalism started out as an accident. The original inventor of the syrup – an Atlanta chemist called John Pemberton – decided to let shops add fizzy water and bottle it if they wanted to, because his syrup's *real* future lay in adding red wine.

Inspired by a drink called Vin Mariani, in the sense that it was the exact same thing, Coca Cola didn't start out as sugar water, but as an invigorating 'heath tonic' called Pemberton's French Wine Cola. Combining wine, cocaine and the caffeine-rich kola nut, it was advertised as an 'intellectual beverage' and a sure-fire cure for nerve trouble, constipation and headaches. It was also 'a most wonderful invigorator of the sexual organs' (something to maybe keep in mind if you still plan on googling porn).

Debuting in 1885, French Wine Cola was a moderate but hardly spectacular success, given that cocaine-laced tonics were pretty thick on the ground. Vin Mariani's fans, after all, were said to include people like the Shah of Persia and King Alphonse of Spain. Pope Leo XIII even gave it a gold medal bearing 'his august effigy' as a 'token of gratitude' for its 'beneficent effects'. Against international brand power such as this, how was a little Southern company to compete? The short answer was that it simply could not.

But then later that first year, everything suddenly changed. The state of Georgia's government decided to bring in Prohibition. Not wanting to face jail, Pemberton instead went back to his recipe book, took the wine out of the recipe, and added cane sugar to what was now a syrup. The result was a thick, sweet, sticky sludge that he decided to call 'Coca Cola'.

His next step was to visit a local shop that sold fizzy soda water from a fountain. He added some to the syrup, decided the results weren't too bad and started selling his syrup to other shops that had a fountain in tow. He saw no point investing in carbonation equipment, a cannery, or even a water supply, because Atlanta's experiment with Prohibition always looked like being short-lived.

And sure enough, it barely lasted a year. Pemberton was able to return to making his French Wine within months, and its sales far outstripped the cheap, sweet syrup he continued to make on the side. He died entirely unaware that his 'invigorating brain tonic' would one day take over the world, along with the somewhat half-arsed way in which he went about making it.

So modern capitalism began with cocaine. And when you think about all those coked-up banker-wankers whose overconfident risk-taking caused the Global Financial Crisis, it may not be too much for a stretch to say that coke might one day help capitalism come to an end.

MEANWHILE, IN AUSTRALIA

A 2017 survey on drug use around the world found some surprising things about Australian habits. For instance, you'll be proud to hear that, while we don't consume the most marijuana, we are world leaders when it comes to using bongs. And while we don't take the most cocaine, we *do* tend to pay the most for it – another fact that may swell some hearts. According to Dr Adam Winstock, the leader of the study, our geographical isolation and tough border control means that we're more likely to hop on the bandwagon of any weird new drugs that come through, using as much as we can before the authorities cotton on and restrict them. The problem is they're often even riskier than the old favourites. A few years ago synthetic cannabis – sold as 'incense' that was 'not for human consumption' – was linked to three mysterious deaths in a four-month period, and the authorities are only just scrambling to close the loopholes that stop these substances being classified as drugs.

CHILLAXANTS

Opium, heroin & dope

Good writing does not always age well. I just read something that I wrote last week, for example, and strictly between us, it was shit.

Even more unreadable, as it happens, was a long passage about opium which I recently came across in a history book. Though on balance this was not unreasonable, since said passage was 6000 years old. A paean to the 'joy plant', and the way it can help to relieve diarrhoea, the Sumerian tablets from Bronze-Age Iraq are just one of many pieces of evidence that ancient people were pretty keen on their poppies.

Want more? Well, 6000-year-old seeds have been found at Palaeolithic burial sites in Switzerland, Germany and Spain. There's evidence that the Egyptians had major poppy fields in around 1300 BCE, and did a roaring trade around the Mediterranean. And if you look at ancient statues, examine ancient pots and, well, google 'ancient opium use', it's clear that Phoenicians, Babylonians and Assyrians also got into the stuff, along with various other *'–ians'* that I'd never heard of. The ancient Greeks even had a whole city that they called Mekonê, or 'Poppy-town'.

I'm betting that city saw its fair share of tourists. Though most would have considered themselves patients, of course, since the joy plant was nothing more than a medicine.

Mind you, it was an unusually *popular* medicine. Galen, the famous Greek physician, was hardly alone in recommending it for just about 'all the pestilences' that could ever plague a man, a list that included 'chronic headache, vertigo, deafness, epilepsy, apoplexy, dimness of sight, loss of voice, asthma, coughs of all kinds, spitting of blood, tightness of breath, colic, the lilac poison, jaundice, hardness of the spleen stone, urinary complaints, fever, dropsies, leprosies [and] the trouble to which women are subject.'

And along with curing just about everything, opium also seemed to be rather enjoyable. Unlike Codral, Panadol or pretty much any other medicine I can think of, it attracted enthusiastic nicknames from long-term 'patients' – nicknames such as 'the milk of paradise' and 'the hand of God'. And 'the destroyer of grief'. And 'the sacred anchor of life'.

Needless to say, this enthusiasm was a little misplaced. Being addictive, a depressant and lethal in large doses, opium could also act as a destroyer of life (or, if you prefer, as a sacred anchor of grief).

So I'm glad to be able to tell you that medical technology progressed. In 1803, opium's active ingredient was finally isolated and turned into a brand new drug called 'morphine'. Named after Morpheus, the Greek God of Dreams, morphine was 'a non-addictive pain medication' to beat all non-addictive pain medications. And its good work became even more widespread with the 1853 invention of the syringe.

Fortunately, this exciting new drug very rapidly fell out of favour.

Unfortunately, the reason was an even *more* exciting new drug with the trademarked name of Heroin™. Synthesised from morphine by Bayer (the German company which also gave us Aspirin), this 'heroic' cough suppressant proved to be a bit too good at suppressing coughs – insofar as it could often suppress a sufferer's breath altogether. Heroin was banned after a couple of decades, but thanks to the black market it's very much here to stay.

So that's the history of the poppy, people. All in all, I'd say that it's a good ad for dope. My personal go-to in the otherwise often grim world of drugs, marijuana is another plant with a long history of 'curing' its patients, or at the very least helping them chill the fuck out.

Though there are healthier ways to get to sleep, of course. I'd suggest reading a Sumerian tablet.

Early evidence of opium use

- c. 6000 BCE – Evidence of opium poppy farming by Neolithic farmers found at La Marmotta, about 20 miles north-west of Rome, Italy
- c. 4000 BCE – Traces of an opium poppy capsule found on the teeth of a male skeleton found in cave near Granada in Spain
- c. 1500 BCE – Opium remnants found in an Egyptian tomb
- c. 700 BCE – Mud and ivory broaches representing poppy capsules found in archaeological excavations on Samos Island in Greece. A broach with the same representation also found in a tomb in the city of Mycenae

Early evidence of marijuana use

- c. 2700 BCE – Chinese medicine book describes hemp's effectiveness in treating the pains of rheumatism and gout
- c. 1550 BCE – The Egyptian *Ebers Papyrus* (one of the world's oldest medical texts) suggests hemp ground in honey inserted in the vagina to treat inflammation
- c. 1213 BCE – Cannabis pollen found on the mummy of Ramesses II
- c. 800-400 BCE – Cannabis 'shroud' discovered placed on a corpse in north-western China, suggesting use in ritual

Nicknames for heroin

- Tar
- Junk
- Brown Sugar
- Skag
- Smack

Nicknames for marijuana

- Pot
- Weed
- Grass
- Ganga
- Skunk

Phrases meaning stoned

- High
- Toasted
- Wasted
- Ripped
- Wrecked

Heroin pros

- A 'rush'
- Reduced sensation of pain
- Feelings of being warm and flushed
- Heavy sensation in the extremities

Heroin cons

- Nausea and vomiting
- Grogginess
- Confusion
- Dry mouth
- Itchy skin

Heroin big-time cons

- ★ Depression
- ★ Decrease in sexual functioning
- ★ Excoriated skin from scratching
- ★ Chronic constipation
- ★ Diminished immune system
- ★ Pulmonary infections

A CONSEQUENTIAL CASH CROP

Is the way we all speak due to dope?

> 'Cannabis's multiple usability might have made it an ideal candidate for being a "cash crop before cash", a plant that is cultivated primarily for exchange purpose.'
>
> Dr Tengwen Long

From Spain to Siberia is a fairly long walk. About 9000 kilometres, I believe, give or take a few steps, so bring water and remember to stretch. And if you zig-zag a bit to take in the sights – all of Europe; most of the Middle East, a bit of India and Bangladesh – you'll end up seeing something like three billion people, and hear them speak in 445 tongues. So maybe pack a few language books too.

You probably don't need 445, though. As a matter of a fact, a few dozen might do, because in some ways all these languages are quite similar.

For example it's an interesting fact (and one only noticed quite recently) that no matter where you might be in Europe or Asia, the local word for 'mother' will probably start with an 'M'. Indians have *maans*, Greeks have *mitéras*, Russians have *mamas* and Iranians have *mātars*.

The English word 'father' is also hardly unique when you consider all the *patĕrs*, *pitárs*, *athirs* and *faders* that stretch out over two continents. An English-speaker's 'brother' is an Icelandic-speaker's *bróðir*, a Latvian's *brālis* and a Bosnian's *brate*. And his sister could just as easily be a *sestra*. Or indeed a *swésor*. Or a *svásar*. Or a *swistar*.

And believe me, friend, that is just the beginning. From plants and animals to everyday verbs, the number of similarities between geographically distinct languages could fill up 445 books in itself.

So what gives? Is this all just coincidence? Or could supernatural forces be in some way involved?

Nope, just historical ones. The fact that, say, Slavs, Kurds and Swedes all have similar words for 'grain', 'tongue' and 'horse' is not actually a surprise when you consider where those words once all came from. Around 10,000 years ago, give or take a few centuries, there lived a huge group of people that we today call the 'Proto-Indo-Europeans'. Mostly based in what's now the Ukraine – i.e. smack-bang in the middle of Eurasia – they seem to have had $meH_2térs$ for mothers and $pH_2térs$ for fathers, as well as $b^hréH_2ters$ and *swésors* and so forth.

Archaeologists are still working out what these people did with their time, but it's pretty clear that at some point they all divided up and started to move. Ever so slowly different tribes spread north, south, east and west, merging their words with the local dialect wherever it was that they finally settled. It was a process that ultimately led to 445 new languages, every single one of them just a bit like the old. In short, Sister Sledge was entirely correct when they sang 'We are family'.

So where do drugs come into all this, you ask? It's a good question; you have been very patient. God's greatest drug, marijuana, might just be the reason why one of these tribes moved.

Que? Well, 'a systematic review of archaeological and paleo-environmental records of cannabis' recently found that Europeans started to plant and smoke *a lot* more dope around about 5000 years ago. 'Carbonised achenes' of marijuana that date back to that time have been found at archaeological sites here, there and everywhere.

What's interesting about this is the date: 5000 years ago. Because that's exactly when we think one of the major Proto-Indo-European tribes decided to spread its wings into what we now all call Europe. Some archaeologists speculate that this 'westward migration of the Yamnaya people further spread the practice of cannabis smoking in Europe'. Dope, they suggest, could well 'be associated with the trans-Eurasian exchange-migration network through the steppe zone'.

Translation: the Yamnaya might have been drug dealers. The founders of European language, culture and civilisation could actually have had quite a lot in common with that dodgy bogan in tracky-daks who keeps hanging around at the end of your street. Tribes wouldn't have had much incentive to trek thousands of miles, after all, if they didn't have something small, light and easy to trade. Meat and vegies go off, cloth's very heavy and the Bronze Age had barely begun.

Cannabis seeds, on the other hand, could just go into a sack (and indeed could be used to make one, if you grew them for hemp). Chances are that dope was Europe's first international currency – the perfect item to trade for food, shelter and land.

Be sure to mention that to your meH$_2$tér if she ever catches you lighting a joint.

GREAT AUSTRALIAN CHILLOUTS

Joseph Banks, 1803

'The Bang you ask for is the powder of the leaves of a kind of hemp that grows in the hot climates. It is prepared, and I believe used, in all parts of the east from Morocco to China. In Europe it is found to act very differently on different constitutions. Some it elevates in the extreme; others it renders torpid … I send a small quantity only as I possess very little. If however, it is found to agree, I will instantly forward the whole of my stock, and write without delay to Barbary, from whence it came, for more.'

The renowned botanist on sending 'bang' to the poet Coleridge.

Burke and Wills, 1863

'They also gave us some stuff they call bedgery, or pedgery. It has a highly intoxicating effect, when chewed even in small quantities … much the same effect as two pretty stiff nobblers of brandy.'

Notes in the doomed explorer Wills's diary describing the 'pituri' provided, along with food and shelter, by an Indigenous tribe at Cooper Creek.

Brett Whiteley, 1969

'Drugs are a phenomenon of the world, just like the atomic bomb.'

The artist attempting to explain the significance of drugs to a journalist for the Sydney Morning Herald.

Joe Cocker, 1972

'There's some around here somewhere.'

The American singer's helpful response to police who had raided his Adelaide hotel room and asked if there was any marijuana in his possession.

THE ANOINTED ONES

Is marijuana a part of the bible?

'Make the most of the Indian hemp seed, and sow it everywhere!'

George Washington

The Bible has lots of commandments: from memory, I think about ten. According to God and his spokesman Moses, thou might recall, thou shalt not kill, steal or commit adultery. Nor should thou run around bearing false witness or coveting thy neighbour's wife, servant, donkey or ox. Making false idols is another big no-no, as is taking the Lord's name in vain.

But next time you're thinking about lighting a joint, you should feel free to go right ahead. There's none of that 'thou shalt not' stuff around dope – in fact it's not mentioned at all.

Or is it?

In amongst all the stories about Adam, Eve, David, Goliath and people with strange names like Nebuchadnezzar, the Old Testament contains several mentions of a plant by the also-strange name of 'calamus'. The books of Exodus, Isaiah, Jeremiah, Ezekiel and Song of Songs all talk about it, but what it *is* remains something of a mystery. All we can really say for certain is that calamus is one of the five ingredients that God tells Moses to use when He's in the mood for some holy anointing. 'Take the following fine spices,' says the Supreme deity: '500 shekels of liquid myrrh, half as much of fragrant cinnamon, 250 shekels of calamus, 500 shekels of cassia, and a hind of olive oil. Make these into a sacred anointing oil, a fragrant blend, the work of a perfumer ... and whatever touches them will be holy.'

Okay, then. What now?

'Anoint Aaron and his sons,' the Big G continues, 'so they may serve me as priests'. He then has Moses splash the stuff over some furniture and set it all alight so as to make an 'alter of incense'. 'Say to the Israelites, this is to be my sacred anointing oil for the generations to come. Do not pour it on men's bodies and do not make any oil with the same formula. It is sacred, and you are to consider it sacred. Whoever makes perfume like it and whoever puts it on anyone other than a priest must be cut off from his people.'

Commanding stuff, you have to agree – and, even though this God fellow never actually existed, very much reflective of what his chosen people chose to do with their time. The word 'Messiah' means 'anointed one'. Without being ceremonially covered in gunk or setting it alight in order to breathe in the smoke, no ancient Israelite could ever hope to be a king, queen or priest. Being anointed with oil was a big step towards holiness and a deep, full and real bond with God.

As religious rituals go, it all seems a bit strange and random – not to mention unpleasant, since this was before soap and showers. The obvious question, then, why did they do this?

The possible answer is one of the ingredients – that ingredient being the mysterious calamus. Some say that it was one of a number of then-common marsh plants (all of which, when burnt, emit quite toxic fumes). The problem is that – since march plants were common and the Israelites didn't use them for much – '250 shekels' would have bought Moses *a whole lot* of calamus. And inhaling all its smoke would have thus made him quite sick. I know that God gave us plague, pestilence and Bernard Tomic, but it seems a little odd for Him to insist that all would-be priests and kings must begin their holy path with an almighty big spew.

Which brings us to Sula Benet. In 1936 that Polish etymologist suggested that the word 'calamus' may actually be a Greek mistranslation of the original Hebrew (hardly an uncommon occurrence when it comes to the Bible). The original word, he controversially suggested, could very easily have been 'kaneh-bosm', a Hebrew phrase that means 'fragrant hemp'. If true, that would mean that Moses and his merry crew really *were* all 'high priests'. It would mean that getting in touch with God simply involved getting stoned.

Whether this is true, we'll just never know, but it would certainly make a whole lot more sense. For one thing, '250 shekels' worth' would start to sound about right, hemp having been a common commercial plant at the time. The ancient Israelis and their neighbours used it to make clothes, ropes, sails, fishnets, and sealant (whatever that was).

And of course they also smoked it – and often smoked in the same way that we now burn incense. As Chris Bennet points out, 'Lacking the invention of pipes, it was the practice of some ancient peoples to burn cannabis and other herbs in tents so that more smoke could be captured and inhaled.'

'Calamus' really being 'cannabis' would also make sense when you look at the way God specifically insists that it be a privilege reserved for his priests – and that they only use it on special occasions. If ordinary Israelites had been getting stoned every day, they would have been wandering the desert for far more than 40 years.

In short, then, it seems that thou shalt not smoke, unless thou art very religious.

NORTH KOREA THE POT HAVEN?

For years rumours have been doing the rounds that North Korea, that most controlling of regimes, actually allows the consumption of marijuana. Stories have been told of huge expanses of wild cannabis being openly harvested and sold in marketplaces, free to be used by all wherever and whenever.

TERRA CANNABIS?

Were the convicts sent here to grow hemp?

> 'Make the most of the Indian Hemp Seed and sow it everywhere.'
>
> George Washington

The *HMS Endeavour* was not a big ship. Roughly the size of a tennis court (if you can imagine a tennis court with 3-metre-high walls), that former coal boat carried no less than 94 passengers on its long voyage to the Great Southern Land. Only the very shortest members of the crew could ever stand up straight below deck, and only the most senior didn't have to sleep in a hammock. It would have been like spending three years in an overcrowded nightclub, only with less music and more chance of scurvy.

Mind you, things might have been a lot roomier had they not insisted on bringing along so much booze. Those 250 beer barrels took up a bit of space below decks, along with those 51 barrels of brandy and rum.

Now, I know what you're thinking: where the hell was the wine? Well don't worry, because Captain Cook thought the same. Four weeks into the voyage (and four tonnes of beer lighter) he stopped by Madeira and purchased 13,650 litres. It's not really all that surprising, in retrospect, that 'several of the *Endeavour*'s crew died from acute alcohol poisoning'.

But for the *real* scandal, perhaps we shouldn't look below deck; perhaps we should look at the sails, ropes and rigging above. Because all of them were made out of cannabis. The world's strongest natural fibre (and the source of the word 'canvas'), hemp was one of planet Earth's most important products back when the Brits ruled the waves. Your average ship-of-the-line needed about 80 tonnes of the stuff – and new sails at least every four years. Without cannabis sativa, British ships simply wouldn't have had the strength to sail across rugged open oceans for weeks, months and years at a time. They wouldn't have been able to carry heavy items to trade livestock or other heavy weapons with which they could conquer.

But just like today (damn you, Australian Government) cannabis wasn't all that easy to come by. And believe me when I say that it's quite hard to grow. Since British hemp growers seemed to find hemp-growing particularly hard, the ever-expending British navy tended to look overseas. For centuries, the American colonies served as a major supplier, with Thomas Jefferson and George Washington just two of many prominent citizens to have a hand in the hemp trade.

But Russian traders were the navy's main source of the stuff – and more or less its *only* source after the US colonies rebelled. And that overreliance on distant Russia was a problem, because plenty of Britain's enemies lay right in its way. All a country such as, say, France had to do to bring Britain's navy to a halt was to waylay a few Russian ships as they sailed past Calais. As Dr John Jiggens rather poetically puts it, after the American revolution of 1776, the British Empire 'dangled by that ribbon of hempen trade that wound its way through the narrow and dangerous passages of the Baltic Sea'.

Which brings us to 1787, the year the First Fleet set sail for Australia. The year that saw an expensive, dangerous and complex voyage carried out purely in order to re-house a few crims. Thinking about it now, it seems just a tiny bit odd. Surely it would have been cheaper and easier to just build a new prison?

For Jiggins, the convict story was simply a cover story. Just as the US army's reliance on oil led it to 'liberate' Kuwait, the actual hidden purpose of the new colony was to provide the navy with a new source of hemp. In his controversial book, *Sir Joseph Banks and the Question of Hemp*, he states, 'My analysis of the hemp trade between 1776 and 1815 shows that the need for a hemp colony was a recurring theme in British strategic thinking during the Georgian era.'

So where does Sir Joseph Banks come into all this? Well – called, as he is, the 'Father of Australia' – there's no doubt that he played a big role in the decision to colonise it. As a close friend of King George, a member of the Privy Council and the man in charge of the Royal Society, he was 'a major influence in the direction and design of British policy', and that country's 'greatest proponent of settlement in New South Wales'.

And he was also a big fan of hemp. That botanist kept a thick file on the best ways and means to grow cannabis, and supervised experimental hemp 'colonies' in India and the Pacific. He gave bagfuls of seeds to folks sailing aboard the First Fleet, and shared hash with chums such as the poet, Samuel Coleridge. It was thanks to Banks's seeds that one NSW governor was able to sow 10 acres of 'Indian hemp' – all of which grew 'with utmost luxuriance, generally from six to ten feet in height.'

But where's the rest, then? The problem with Jiggins's theory, of course, is that when it comes to cannabis cultivation in 18th-century Oz, those 10 acres were more or less it. If *Terra Australis* was really intended to be *Terra Cannabis*, wouldn't the convicts have ... you know ... actually grown some?

Jiggins's explanation for this rather large hole in his theory is that, while 'hemp formed the basis for war, trade, and empire in that early period of mercantile capitalism ... coal took over [very soon after the First Fleet)] and became strategic in the same way'. Cannabis motivated the British to come here, in other words, but – once they actually got here – it became obsolete.

Well ... maybe. Or maybe the truth lies somewhere in between. As the University of Melbourne's Trevor Burnard puts it, 'most historians would not say that it was only hemp that led to Botany Bay, but that growing hemp was a consideration alongside creating a convict colony.'

ANOTHER KIND OF 'WEED'

While Australia may not have become the heart of the world cannabis trade, attempts to grow hemp in the Great Southern Land weren't *entirely* fruitless. In fact some of the cannabis crops planted in the Hunter Valley during the 1800s were so successful that, by 1963 they were sprouting wild along river banks and irrigation channels, just waiting to be harvested by entrepreneurial tourists. Australia's marijuana consumption boomed in the '60s, and local dairy farmers were soon complaining about the groups of flower children that kept traipsing through their paddocks every autumn. It took authorities nine years to clear the 'infestation,' which at its height covered 30 square kilometres.

Oh, the waste, the tragic waste. Let's all take a moment to mourn.

MOTHER'S LITTLE HELPER

The 'medicine' that killed millions of kids

'Among the remedies which it has pleased Almighty God to give to man to relieve his sufferings, none is so universal and so efficacious as opium.'

— Thomas Sydenham

To 'take your medicine' these days is to endure something bad, but once upon a time it must have been rather pleasant.

I refer of course to the West's golden age of healing: to that 100-or-so-year period, starting around 1810, when just about every ailment could be treated with opium. It was an age when people with colds didn't have to soldier on with Codral, but could instead take a soothing puff on a pipe.

While the poppy has been used since ancient times to deaden pain – and make patients, if not precisely 'well', then feel good – its widespread use in the Western world didn't really kick off until the 1700s. What happened then was that the Brits took over India and started to exploit every square inch of it, as at the time was their want. Finding themselves in possession of a climate that was perfectly suited to poppy-growing and full of poverty-stricken farmers who they could brutally exploit, the next step for the British was to convert vast swathes of farmland into 'efficiently' run poppy fields, turn the result into opium and offload it across the globe.

By 1850 British consumers alone were buying 138,000 kilos a year. By 1870 the government's profits from said worldwide trade accounted for no less than a fifth of Britain's entire revenue. The Empire over which the sun never set was basically a drug cartel with a flag.

But it's not like every customer was sitting in an opium den and puffing away on a pipe – most patients took their medicine in the form of *actual* medicine. Whether you had asthma, the sniffles, a sore throat or a strange rash, opium-laced products didn't just 'invigorate the nervous system', they could also 'assuage pain of every kind'.

All these medicines were *so* great, in fact, that people often had them when they weren't even ill. In 1873 one English physician wrote about the peculiar way in which 'the crowds in the chemists' shops come for opium' – a way which seemed to imply that these patients hadn't come straight from a doctor.

'They go in, lay down their money and receive the opium pills in exchange without saying a word. [One evening, I] went into a chemist's shop and laid a penny on the counter. The chemist said "The best?"

I nodded. He gave me a pill box and took up the penny; and so the purchase was completed without my having uttered a syllable. You offer money and get opium as a matter of course ... In these districts it is taken by people of all classes, but especially by the poor and miserable, and by those who in other districts would seek comfort from gin or beer.'

But let's not suggest that *everyone* bought Batley's Sedative Solution and the like for some kind of cheap, sordid high. That would be profoundly unfair, for they also bought it in order to shut up their kids. Complementing the opium with morphine sulphate (and up to 45 per cent alcohol), products like Mother Bailey's Quieting Syrup were able to do so much more than cure pretty much every childhood disease on the planet (including 'colic, diarrhoea, vomiting, hiccups, pleurisy, rheumatism, catarrhs, and cough'). They were also able to help your kids get to sleep, and to be more docile whenever they were awake. '[It] was like magic,' said one mother in a letter to the *Times*. Her teething infant 'soon went to sleep, and all pain and nervousness disappeared'.

Opium-laced treacle was also a popular kid's treat in Britain, where sweet sticks were sold at a penny a pop. One doctor reported that several of his child patients were 'shrank up into little old men' and looked 'wizened like little monkeys'.

Now I'm not doctor or anything, but that doesn't sound like a good sign. Another bad sign was the high rates of infant mortality. As anyone who's ever read a Dickens novel knows, childhoods back in the Victorian era weren't just nasty and brutish, they were very often cut quite short. And while not too many kids died from a direct overdose of 'medicine', that doesn't mean that their 'tonics' weren't deadly.

As a Privy Council investigation subsequently noted, children 'kept in a state of continued narcotism will be thereby disinclined for food, and be but imperfectly nourished'. Translation: being in an opium haze makes a baby a lot less inclined to breastfeed, and a little kid eat much less than they should. Malnutrition was one of the Victorian world's biggest killers, and eating opium treacle probably wasn't much help.

MEANWHILE, IN AUSTRALIA

In the 1830s Australia was very much still a part of the British Empire. So it was tied up in all British interests – including their insatiable craving for opium-based medicines. In fact, the Australian Agricultural Company, a consortium of influential British politicians and public servants, had well-developed plans to grow poppies in Australia, but those plans were never realised. Being patriotic souls, we all like to support local industry. But it may not, on the whole, be such a bad thing that we never had home-grown versions of such popular products as Godfrey's Cordial, Dover's Powder, Dalby's Carminative, McMunn's Elixir and Atkinson's Royal Infants Preservative.

A NOBLE CAUSE

The four-year war fought over opium

> 'Junk is the ideal product... the ultimate merchandise. No sales talk necessary. The client will crawl through a sewer and beg to buy.'
>
> William S Burroughs

I'm pretty sure I'd be brave enough to be a soldier were it not for the fact that war can get you hurt and/or killed. With all those bullets flying around and bombs going off, you're liable to lose a limb that you'd much rather have kept, or get shot in a sensitive region. If conscription ever came back, I'd probably push for some sort of admin-type role, though even *then* you're at risk of a paper cut.

Is it any wonder, then, that some soldiers have turned to the poppy after a long day of being stabbed, bashed and maimed? Supposedly used during the Trojan War and by the Spartans when they fought against Athens, poppy juice really came into its own during the US Civil War, by which time it had been turned into morphine. Used as anaesthetic in operations, and as a way to reduce chronic pain, this 'wonder drug' became so common during the four-year-long conflict that some 400,000 soldiers finished it up as addicts.

Thankfully things had improved when US soldiers found themselves in Vietnam a century later. Though the 'improvement' in this case was that soldiers were now using heroin, a much stronger and more fast-acting high. When Richard Nixon declared a 'war on drugs' – a war that most of the Western world is still 'fighting' today – the very first shot that he fired, so to speak, was the introduction of compulsory urine testing for all troops in Nam. The Pentagon estimates that 45 per cent of Vietnam vets used some kind of drug, and 15 per cent became addicted to heroin.

But it's one thing for opiates to fuel a war by helping the people in it to cope. It's quite another for opiates to *cause* one.

And it turns out that they actually have.

In the early 1800s the British Empire was still a thing – and you didn't have to tell this to Indians. Always on the lookout for new ways to exploit the natives, Queen Victoria et al really hit the jackpot when they took over the fertile poppy fields of the Ganges plain. Grown for next to nothing by locals who the British were prepared to pay even less, it really would have been the perfect product ... were it not for a shortage of customers.

Europeans, you see, were only just starting to wake up to the poppy's endless medical potential. Opium-laced syrups, tinctures, injections and pills were not yet the bustling pharmaceutical industry that they were destined to one day become. So the Brits decided to sell opium in China instead. Or rather to smuggle it in, given the stuff was illegal. A country with a long history of recreational use and abuse, thanks to ancient trade links with what's now Afghanistan, China really didn't need 40,000 barrels of opium pouring in through its borders each year, but thanks to the British, that was just what it got.

By 1838 the Empire had millions of reliable customers: China had become a nation of addicts, with predictably disastrous results. 'The army became corrupt', the bureaucracy 'declined in efficiency', 'business activity was much reduced', and the economy slowly ground to a halt. 'Opium is a poison,' Emperor Jiaqing declared. '[It is] undermining our good customs and morality.'

In 1839 the mandarins finally took action, seizing 20,000 barrels of true-blue British and throwing the good folk who'd smuggled it in into prison.

Clearly, this meant war. Outraged that honest Chinese workers were to be denied this 'harmless luxury', the British promptly attacked the port city of Canton (now Guangzhou) – and kept on attacking for the best part of four years, causing 'untold casualties and deaths'.

Untold *Chinese* casualties and deaths, that is. Given the difference in wealth, weapons and training, the First Opium War was not what you'd call a fair fight. (Imagine the US invading Tahiti today. Or, I don't know, pretty much anyone in a fight with Grant Denyer.)

As one journalist wrote about a typical 'battle' – that battle being

Britain's brutal sack of Chusan – 'a more complete pillage could not be conceived ... Every house was broken open, every drawer and box ransacked, the streets strewn with fragments of furniture, pictures, tables, chairs, grain of all sorts – the whole set off by the dead or the living bodies of those who had been unable to leave the city from the wounds received from our merciless guns ... The plunder ceased only when there was nothing to take or destroy.'

The end result of the First Opium War was that the British got the vital port of Hong Kong, along with five other territories in which to ply their trade. The Chinese also had to pay the poor old Empire for the three-and-half-years' worth of opium it would have otherwise have sold them. These people certainly knew how to rub salt in the wound, and then add petrol and set it alight.

DON'T BLAME THE CHINESE

Plenty of Chinese emigrants to colonial Australia used to smoke opium, but it ought to go without saying that they were hardly alone. Very much legal in Australia at the time, and a staple ingredient in patent medicines, the poppy had many more Aussie users back then than today – and the majority of them were white, middle class women.

FRANKENSTEIN'S MONSTER

Was the world's first great horror novel inspired by a trip?

'If you want your tree to produce plenty o' fruit, you've got to cut it back from time to time. Same thing with your neural cells. Some people might call it brain damage. I call it prunin'.'

Tom Robbins

We all have bad dreams from time to time. My own tend to involve nasty flashbacks. That time when I went scuba diving and saw a big shark, for example. Or worse, that time I saw *Zoolander II*.

You'd have to hope that Mary Shelley's nightmares were a bit less based in reality. Living in the early 1800s would have been hard enough without having to encounter a bunch of dead people's body parts stitched together into the shape of a man. I'm talking about a 'hideous corpse' with 'watery eyes', 'straight black lips' and 'yellow skin'. A hideous corpse that, 'upon the working of some powerful engine' operated by some 'pale student of unhallowed arts', suddenly stirs and shows signs of life.

Fortunately, Mary Shelley had never actually seen such a thing (plastic surgery not having hit Hollywood). The 'frightful' dream that inspired the then-18-year-old to write *Frankenstein* was just that and no more: a dream.

Or *sort of* a dream. 'When I placed my head on my pillow, I did not sleep, nor could I be said to think,' said the writer years later of that dark, stormy night – a night she famously spent on the shores of Lake Geneva, where she and assorted writer pals had all rented a cosy cottage. 'My imagination, unbidden, possessed and guided me, gifting the successive images that arose in my mind with a vividness far beyond the usual bounds of reverie.'

So a sort of *awake* dream, then? Hmmm. Without wanting to in any way leap to conclusions, is it possible that what she had was a trip?

What if I was to tell you that Shelley's stay in Geneva coincided with a massive volcanic eruption in the East Indies, a climatic event which spewed ash so far north that even in Europe it was cold, dark and windy? 'An almost perpetual rain confines us principally to the house,' Mary wrote in a letter home during what became known as 'the year without a summer'. She and her companions entertained themselves by reading from a book of ghost stories they'd found lying around the cottage, and challenging each other to write stories of their own.

And what if I added that two of those companions were Lord Byron, a man who was never far from his opium pipe, and Mary's husband, Percy Bysshe Shelley, who kept his equally close. They weren't just 'the most brilliant and romantic circle of poets, writers and personalities which Switzerland has ever seen', as Elma Dangerfield once put it, they were also amongst the most drug-addled. In particular, they were prone to use laudanum, a sort of liquid opium designed to cure every ill.

On the night that Mary had her fateful dream, her husband had swallowed way too much of the stuff. Close observers could tell this by the way he became convinced that Mary's nipples had been replaced by huge demonic eyes, and so leapt up and ran shrieking from their room. So is it *really* such an enormous stretch to suggest that his wife might have had a sip or two herself?

If she did, then we largely owe *Frankenstein* to opium – and its contribution to the horror genre may not even stop there. Another of the ghost stories produced during that house-bound holiday came from the pen of Dr John Polidori, Lord Byron's 'personal physician' – an opium addict who eventually killed himself. Featuring a dark, brooding, aristocratic bloodsucker (not unlike the dark and brooding Lord B), *The Vampyre* had a great deal in common with *Dracula*, except for the fact that it was published about 80 years earlier.

SONGS ABOUT HALLUCINOGENS

There's no inspiration like hallucination, as these songs all suggest.

- 'Purple Haze' (Jimi Hendrix)
- 'Legend of a Mind' (The Moody Blues)
- '2,000 Light Years From Home' (The Rolling Stones)
- 'Sunshine Superman' (Donovan)
- 'And She Was' (Talking Heads)

A SPOT OF ENCHANTMENT

Great writers who were on less-than-great drugs

'Find what you like, and let it kill you.'

Kinky Friedman

There's nothing particularly romantic about opiates these days, unless you happen to be turned on by syringes and the slim chance of disease. But back in what's now called the Romantic Age – that time when it was okay for straight men to wear velvet tights – taking opiates was not just de rigueur. If you were a poet or a writer, it was pretty close to compulsory.

Coleridge didn't need telling twice. For that poet, the opium pipe offered 'sweet repose' in a place that was simply 'divine'. It took him to 'a spot of enchantment', as he once told his brother: to 'a green spot of fountains and flowers and trees in the very heart of a waste of sands.'

For Keats, in contrast, it was more about the wasted lungs: swigging laudanum offered a level of respite from the tuberculosis that ended up killing him at just 25. 'Ode to a Nightingale' and 'Ode on Indolence' are thought to have been written under its influence, much like Coleridge's iconic 'The Rime of the Ancient Mariner' and 'Kubla Khan'.

Shelley, for his part, used it to 'dampen the nerves', though apparently not with too much success. After years of 'body spasms,' 'haunting dreams' and 'confusions about reality,' the poet was advised by his doctor to stop using it. Naturally Shelley told him to get stuffed.

Shelley also used laudanum for romantic purposes – so long as you think telling your teenage ex to commit suicide is 'romantic'. After the young couple were separated by her (not unreasonably) concerned parents, Shelley broke into her house brandishing a bottle of laudanum and a pistol and told her to drain the former, right then and there. 'By this you can escape from tyranny,' that tights-wearer thundered. 'They wish to separate us, my beloved; but Death shall unite us.' She didn't go for the whole suicide pact thing, rather unromantically, but they *did* end up running away together, so perhaps it wasn't such a bad strategy.

Anyway, moving on. Because it's not just poets who enjoyed a few moments of repose; plenty of actual, proper writers have had some as well. Four-hundred-year old traces of cannabis have been found in Stratford-upon-Avon, for example, inside clay pipes at Shakespeare's old home. That playwright also wrote about 'a noted weed' in one of his sonnets, and suggested that it could be used as source of 'invention'.

Oscar Wilde also enjoyed a spot of hashish, describing it as 'quite exquisite' in a letter to friends. 'Three puffs of smoke and then peace and love,' he wrote, close to a century before the 1960s. The child of an alcoholic, and perhaps one himself, Wilde also 'never stopped smoking opium-tainted Egyptian cigarettes' according to one of his friends – and it was a habit that he shared with Proust. Another noted 'weed', so to speak, that pale, spindly Frenchman rarely got out of bed before three, and would then immediately start puffing on an opium cigarette in order to alleviate his asthma. It's a habit that could explain why he went *In Search of Lost Time*, and then took so many fucking pages to find it. Such a long, dreamily reflective and endlessly nuanced novel could never have been written by someone on coke.

Who else? Well, it's probably safe to say that Wilkie Collins wrote the world's first detective novel, *The Moonstone*, while under the influence of opium, because there was rarely a time when he wasn't. 'Who was the man who invented laudanum?' that confirmed addict once wondered. 'I thank him from the bottom of my heart.'

Wilkie's best friend and fellow writer is also said to have been partial to the poppy, though this may all just be smoke and no pipe. The only real evidence for the claim that Charles Dickens was prone to 'retire at the end of a long day's writing to puff on a hookah' is the intimate knowledge of the 'sleep and stupor' involved that he shows off in *The Mystery of Edwin Drood*, his uncannily specific, half-finished final novel set in an opium den.

The suggestion that Dickens was a 'laudanum addict' also seems a little far-fetched. But being (probably) bipolar, and in constant pain from a train accident, that author certainly used the stuff more than he should have. Whether or not his stroke at age 58 was the direct result of an overdose, all that daily swigging wouldn't have helped.

Every bit as unhealthy was Elizabeth Barrett Browning, the English creator of *Prometheus Bound*, and assorted other poems that I like to pretend I've read. A laudanum user from the age of 13, when doctors recommended it for a pain in her neck, Browning was hopelessly addicted by the time she hit adulthood and essentially spent the rest of her life in an opium haze. '[I] long to live by myself ... in a forest of chestnuts and cedars, in an hourly succession of poetical paragraphs and morphine draughts,' she once wrote in a letter to her brother. And apart from the 'by herself in a forest of chestnuts' bit, you'd have to say that she managed it.

MEANWHILE, IN AUSTRALIA

Australian *artistes* were by no means exempt from this fascination with drugs. Marcus Clarke, author of For the Term of His Natural Life was a famous proponent of getting off your face in order to get a good idea in your brain. He was part of the Yorick Club, a group of Melburnian writers and journalists who liked to gather together to talk self-importantly about literature and pretend to listen when anyone else did the same. They liked to smoke a bit of weed to get the conversation flowing, and Clarke in particular was adamant that marijuana, particularly when eaten, was an ideal source of inspiration. To prove this, he once conducted an 'experiment' in which he ate some hashish and wrote a story called 'Cannabis Indica' while a doctor recorded his actions and comments.

THE SPARKLING FLOOD

Did drugs help create children's literature?

'The Caterpillar took the hookah out of its mouth and yawned once or twice, and shook itself. Then it got down off the mushroom, and crawled away in the grass, merely remarking as it went, "One side will make you grow taller, and the other side will make you grow shorter."'

Lewis Carroll

Much like little kids themselves, the genre of 'children's literature' is really quite young. While fairy tales, fables, funny poems and so forth have all been told for thousands of years, their target audience always included adults, and they tended to dwell on death, pain and disease.

It was only in the early 1800s that the concept of 'childhood' really started to emerge, along with books that were written just for it. And even then, they were all still a bit on the grim side: strict morality tales designed to produce pious citizens; the literary equivalent of a bowl of boiled cabbage The characters in early Victorian literature didn't play so much as pray – as well as study hard and mind their manners. Children's books were still for adults, whether or not adults actually read them.

But this all changed in 1865, with a work you might know called *Alice in Wonderland*. Generally credited with being the first real children's book, *Alice* essentially created a whole new genre: colourful, off-beat kid's stuff written simply to entertain. It was soon followed by *The Wonderful Wizard of Oz*, and then came *Peter Pan*. Crazy nonsense, all three books, but also crazily fun.

So what opened the floodgates? Well it might be worth pointing out that what's known as 'the Golden Age of Children's Literature' was also a golden age for opiates; an age where pretty much everyone was on some kind of 'medicine'.

To explain, here's a quote from *The Electric Kool-Aid Acid Test*, a (very much adult) work written by Tom Wolfe in 1968. 'In ordinary perception,' he writes, 'the senses send an overwhelming flood of information to the brain, which the brain then filters down to a trickle it can manage for the purpose of survival in a highly competitive world. Man has become so rational, so utilitarian, that the trickle becomes most pale and thin. It is efficient, for mere survival, but it screens out the most wondrous parts of man's potential experience without his even knowing it. We're shut off from our own world. Primitive man once experienced the rich and sparkling flood of the senses fully. Children experience it for a few months – until "normal" training, conditioning, close the doors on this other world, usually for good.'

Sad, but here's the good news, folks: 'Somehow ... drugs [can open] these ancient doors.' Taking drugs, in other words, may not make you more employable, or do a great deal for your skin, teeth or sex life. But maybe, just *maybe*, it can give you a glimpse of all the strange and swirling sensations that you haven't had since you were just a kid.

So did *Alice* emerge from the sparkling flood? Well, let's take a look at the evidence. First, the character falls down a hole into a psychedelic and colourful world where time slows down, eccentric animals talk and a drowsy caterpillar smokes some stuff from a hookah. Then Alice shrinks after eating a strange mushroom and plays croquet using a flamingo for a mallet. Then she grows again after eating a cake, whose flavour changes with every chew. There's also a queen who keeps on changing shape, a cat who turns invisible, endless riddles and a (very) Mad Hatter.

Is it so surprising, then, that 'Alice' has become a nickname for LSD, and 'Alice in Wonderland Syndrome' the name of a hallucinatory disease? Is it so surprising that *Alice* inspired Jefferson Airplane's psychedelic album *White Rabbit*, together with the Beatles' most trippy track. 'The images were from *Alice in Wonderland*, it was Alice in the boat,' said John Lennon of 'Lucy in the Sky with Diamonds', that song with tangerine trees, marmalade skies and rocking-horse people who eat marshmallow pies.

While we don't know for sure whether Lewis Carroll took laudanum, what we *do* know that he suffered severe migraines. So it would have been kind of odd if he didn't.

What about *The Wonderful Wizard*? Well, can I remind you that the city of Oz is surrounded by a thick field of poppies – 'bright red flowers' whose 'odour is so powerful that anyone who breathes it falls asleep'. And can I also remind you that when Dorothy does just that, the Good Witch of the North can only revive her by covering her up in a thick blanket of snow. 'Snow,' of course, has long been another word for cocaine, a substance which can be quite reviving.

And *Peter Pan*? Well, its author also had health problems – namely, insomnia and a bad set of lungs. But I'm pleased to report that, it being the early years of the 20th century and all, he didn't seem to rely on laudanum to relieve them. Why would you bother using that primitive old medicine when you could take this brand new, exciting product called 'heroin'?

HIGH AS A WALLABY

'Bright red flowers' aren't just found in the fictional Land of Oz, they're found in the real one too. Tasmania, that island at the bottom of the country, is actually on top of the world when it comes to the legal drug trade: 50 per cent of the world's legal opium is grown there, and it's a fact that some animals have noticed. In 2009, Tassie poppy farmers reported that a number of strange 'crop circles' were starting to pop up all around their farms. After some investigation, it turned out that the cause was not aliens but local wallabies, who were eating into the poppy crops, getting high and hopping around in circles.

Nobody knows why the opium seemed to make the animals move in circles, but farmers have since reported that sheep who accidentally break into their poppy fields often do the same thing.

THE DAYS THE MUSIC DIED

The rock stars who had too much heroin

'For art to exist, for any sort of aesthetic activity or perception to exist, a certain physiological precondition is indispensable: intoxication.'

Friedrich Nietzsche

There are all sorts of ways to live a long life (albeit a long life that you don't really enjoy). They include lengthy walks and daily sessions in the gym, doing yoga and eating tofu and kale.

But what they *don't* include, according to the latest research, is injecting smack straight into your arm. It's counterintuitive, I know, but the evidence seems to suggest that, on balance, it's not great for your body. Who would have thought that a product with names like 'Hell Dust', 'Holy Terror', and 'Dead on Arrival' could cause users to convulse and die?

If junkies were just bankers and real estate agents, this wouldn't necessarily be such a problem. But that sort, alas, tends to prefer safer highs, like exorbitant fees and cocaine. Historically speaking, it's rock stars who tend to get on the horse. And then fall off and get trampled to death.

Edgy and glamorous (if you like sweat, scabs and pale skin), heroin is 'the perfect drug for live performing', as an anonymous rocker once told *Spin*. 'With the right amount, it just relaxes you, but it doesn't take your muscle coordination away.' And it also seems to be the perfect drug for when you're not performing. For all those long, dull days in between live shows; for all that endless down time involved in life on the road. As a slightly less anonymous rocker called Courtney Love once put it, skag is 'the drug you do if you're in a fuckin' four-star hotel and you can order all the goddamn room service that you want and you can just lay in bed and drool all over yourself because you've got a million bucks in the bank. That's the drug you want to do if you want to be a kid forever.'

And it also helps if you want to die young. An early death can be a good career move in rock and roll circles, and if you don't believe me, just go see the still-alive Beach Boys. Musicians who overdosed over the years include Billy Murcia of the New York Dolls and Brent Mydland of the Grateful Dead. Pete Farndon from the Pretenders is no longer with us, just like John Bonham of Led Zeppelin, Shannon Hoon of Blind Melon and John Belushi, the part-time Blues Brother.

Sid Vicious was perhaps less of a loss (and if you don't believe me, just ask the girlfriend he murdered). But Layne Staley of Alice in Chains has a place in rock heaven, just like Amy Winehouse and Janis Joplin.

Two other members of the 27 Club will be there, too, though it's not necessarily clear if they left Earth through heroin. Brian Jones of the Rolling Stones was famously found dead at the bottom of his pool late at night in July 1969. It seems pretty likely that heroin helped put him there, given his history with the drug, and the fact that his heart and liver were both badly swollen. But you'll find plenty of people who insist he was murdered, and still others who will say it was suicide.

Jim Morrison, too, almost certainly died from an OD. But we'll never know for sure because there wasn't an inquest. Again, you get people who insist it was murder – or, even more far-fetched, that he's still alive.

Live fast, die young and leave a beautiful corpse? I think I'd rather grow old and watch telly, even if that has to involve eating tofu and kale.

A CREATIVE VEIN

The classic(al) tunes that have been shaped by smack

'There are many artists whose creativity is almost like madness, but not quite. In conditions like schizophrenia, you have thoughts that are jumbled together that don't necessarily belong together – you have tangential thinking, and thoughts go in bizarre directions, which might be helpful with coming up with bizarre ideas. Part of creativity is being original. So drugs like cocaine, and perhaps heroin, have that ability to make you have original thoughts.'

Dr Alain Dagher

It's quiz time, people. What do these five songs have in common: 'Golden Brown' by the Stranglers, 'There She Goes' by the La's, 'Space Oddity' by David Bowie, 'Under the Bridge' by the Red Hot Chili Peppers, and 'Lust for Life' by Iggy Pop?

Struggling? Then I'll give you a clue. They're all songs about a certain product; a product that is also the subject of 'Perfect Day' by Lou Reed and of Pink Floyd's 'Comfortably Numb'.

Still struggling? I'm thinking cryptic lyrics aren't really your thing. Maybe try listening to 'Heroin' instead. It's not one of the Velvet Underground's better songs, but there's no way you could call it ambiguous.

Anyway, my point here is that it's not – or at least shouldn't be – any great sort of secret that lots of rock songs were inspired by brown tar. The Rolling Stones arguably wrote their best stuff when Keith was on heroin, and the same goes for Bob Dylan and Eric Clapton, not to mention Aerosmith and Ween. '[Heroin] freed me up,' Blur's Damon Albarn once said of his own 'incredibly productive' days shooting up. 'I hate talking about this because of my daughter, my family. But for me it was incredibly creative ... [and] changed me completely as a musician. I found a sense of rhythm. I somehow managed to break out of something with my voice.'

Plenty of jazz musicians have also got on the junk, though Miles Davis managed to kick it after roughly four years. Billie Holiday, on the other hand, was a fully fledged addict. She was arrested repeatedly, and at one point imprisoned, before dying at age 44.

And there's no doubt that Charlie Parker's heroin addiction helped turn him into a genius, according to at least one biographer. 'The truly astounding aspect of this period of his life is how the onset of addiction coincided with such a quantum leap in his musical abilities,' asserts Martin Torgoff. 'Charlie Parker became famous as a man who was perfectly capable of spending a whole day in his hotel room, draining a fifth of whiskey as a reefer dangled from his lip, jacking heroin into a vein while a woman knelt between his legs. And then he would get on a stage and ... take transcendent flight in music of such natural originality and power that it would leave his fellow musicians dumbstruck with wonder.'

By the late 1940s 'the strange and compelling myth was spreading that heroin could make you play like Bird [Parker]', writes Torgoff. 'In Los Angeles, the first three notes of [the Parker classic] "Parker's Mood", whistled into the night, became the code signal among musicians that they wanted to [buy drugs].'

'Every drug has a nature,' is how the Clash's Joe Strummer once explained it. And while it's not great for drumming (or, needless to say, general health), heroin tends to 'suit horn playing, because you can float over the music'.

But what if you want to play piano like Chopin? Heroin might just help with that, too. A surprising fact about staid old classic music is that many of its creators spent their lives smashed. Being a lifelong sufferer from some sort of lung disease (to this day, no one precisely knows which), Chopin was one composer who 'frequently took opiates', according to his biographer, Dr Victoria Wapf. Prone to mixing them with 'virtually anything available: sugar, alcohol, mercury, hashish, cayenne pepper, ether, chloroform, belladonna, and so on', it's not hard to work out why he constantly complained of strange visions before dying at 39. And it's equally easy to see why so many of his compositions tend to be described as 'dreamlike and haunting'.

Who else? Well, Stravinsky was also prone to conduct concerts on opium (when he wasn't performing 'countless unsuccessful experiments with behaviour modification drugs'). And there's a good reason why Berlioz's groundbreaking *Symphonie Fantastique* has been described as 'the first ever musical description of a trip'.

It clearly wasn't the last.

FAREWELL ...

So that's it, folks, welcome to journey's end – at least as far as we know. I've done my best to put together a 'Tanked' theory of history, but perhaps this is only the tip of the iceberg, so to speak, and countless other illicit secrets still wait to be found. After all, if this book teaches you one thing about humanity, it's that we love to get off our faces.

For instance, I've heard that the Minister for ███████ is a bit of a cokehead, and that the guy behind ███████████ likes his crack. But apparently I can't tell you the details because of something called 'libel', and my editor's insistence on this thing she calls 'truth'.

Anyway, I hope that the non-blanked-out bits are true enough. Dipping a toe into the murky waters of human actions and motives is always going to be a ... erm ... murky business, in which no answer is ever quite clear. Who really knows why each of us does what we do, or why anyone else ever did what they did? 'All I know is that I know nothing' as someone once said (see: I don't even know *that*). It's almost enough to make you give up on history and go smoke a joint.

In fact ... I might stop typing here.

THANKS ...

To Tim, Adam, Libby, Bill, Marita, Jen and Tom: wonderful friends, one and all, and great company late at night in a pub.

Thanks are due again to the ever-professional Affirm Press – particularly proofreader Cosima McGrath, and ever-excellent editor Ruby Ashby-Orr. Thanks also to Nanette Backhouse at Saso Creative for the cover design, Renee Bahr at Post Pre-Press Group for the typesetting.